BY EVE ENSLER

I Am an Emotional Creature
A Memory, a Monologue, a Rant, and a Prayer (editor)
Insecure at Last
The Good Body
Necessary Targets
The Vagina Monologues

A Memory, a Monologue, a Rant, and a Prayer

EDITED BY

Eve Ensler

and Mollie Doyle

VILLARD NEW YORK

A Memory,
a Monologue,
a Rant,
and a Prayer

A Villard Trade Paperback Original
Copyright © 2007 by Lotus Productions, Inc.

Published in the United States by Villard Books,
an imprint of The Random House Publishing Group,
a division of Random House, Inc., New York.

VILLARD and "V" CIRCLED Design are registered
trademarks of Random House, Inc.

V-DAY and UNTIL THE VIOLENCE STOPS are trademarks of V-Day.

Owing to limitations of space, copyright credits for the contributions
to this work can be found on pages 221–23.

ISBN 978-0-345-49791-8

LIBRARY OF CONGRESS CATALOGING-IN-PUBLICATION DATA
A memory, a monologue, a rant, and a prayer / edited by Eve Ensler
and Mollie Doyle.
p.   cm.
ISBN 978-0-345-49791-8
1. Women—Violence against. 2. Girls—Violence against.
3. Family violence. 4. Women—Violence against—Literary collection.
5. Girls—Violence against—Literary collection.
6. Family violence—Literary collection. I. Ensler, Eve.
II. Doyle, Mollie.
HV6250.4.W65M437 2007
362.82'920922—dc22   2007001330

Printed in the United States of America

www.villard.com

9

Book design by Dana Leigh Blanchette

*We dedicate this book
to Peace.*

Contents

Rant

Prayer

Contents

Introduction

Eve Ensler

Words. Words. This book is indeed about words. Speaking the unspoken. Speaking the spoken in a new and viable way, speaking the pain, speaking the hunger. Speaking. Speaking about violence against women not because it is the only issue, but because it is an issue that lives smack in the middle of the world and is still not spoken, not seen, not given weight or significance. So that words crack open numbness and denial and disassociation and distance and deception. Speaking so that we are in community, in conscience, in concern.

Speaking about violence against women because in 2006, young Amish girls are gunned down in their school just because they are girls; women are trafficked like meat sold from poor neighborhoods to men in rich neighborhoods; women are raped in Darfur on their way to get wood for the fire or grass for their donkeys. In 2006 women are burned and mutilated and stoned and dismissed and undone and refused and silenced. Speaking about violence because in early November 2006 the president of Israel stepped down after being accused of rape and harassment, and a cleric in Australia blamed uncovered women for getting raped. Speaking about violence against women because of your mother, your sister, your aunt, your daughter, your girlfriend, your best friend, your wife. Speaking about violence against women because the story of women is the story of life itself. In speaking about it, you cannot avoid speaking about racism and domination, poverty and patriarchy, empire building, war, sexuality, desire, imagination. The mechanism of violence is what destroys women, controls women, diminishes women, and keeps them in their so-called place. Speaking about violence, telling the stories, because in the telling, we legitimize women's experience. We reveal what is happening in the dark, in the basement, out of sight. In the telling, women take their power back. Their voice. Their remembering. Their future.

As part of a two-week "Until the Violence Stops" festival held in New York City in the summer of 2006, we asked a group of remarkable writers to contribute memories, monologues, rants, and prayers on the subject of violence against women. We envisioned a pivotal event in which these monologues would be performed by great actors. We thought maybe, maybe, ten or twenty would respond. We were overwhelmed with contributions.

Each writer brought something so specific, so original, so Edward Albee it could only be Edward Albee, so Alice Walker it could only be Alice Walker, so Erin Cressida Wilson, so Michael Eric Dyson.

We need writers in these terrible times of deception and manipulation and sound bites and half-investigated truths, in these times when the lust for power has trumped the hunger for justice, in these times of evildoers and saints. We don't have many real leaders, we don't have many politicians we can trust. But we can trust writers. Rather than selling us something, they are exploring something; rather than dominating us, they are opening us; rather then winning or having a position, they are inviting us to ask questions.

We need each and every writer, each and every artist, to tell the truth the way she or he sees it, the way it comes through her or him. Some of the work in this book is funny, some mysterious, some very difficult, some devastating. All of it is new. The first time it was performed was at the festival before two thousand people. It was thrilling.

The writers in this book received no payment for this work other than the deep satisfaction that comes from serving the higher good. My proceeds and the writers' royalties from the sale of *A Memory, a Monologue, a Rant, and a Prayer* will benefit V-Day. (To find out more about V-Day, see page 191; you can also visit www.v-day.org.)

I thank these great playwrights, poets, journalists, visionaries, for the gift of this book, and I thank you, the reader, for taking this journey.

Memory

Looking for the Body Music

Michael Klein

My friend Frank calls it *looking for the body* music—the music
    my mother heard.
At the end of *looking for the body* music, one stumbles upon a
    woman's body
with the whole world taken out of her—but before that scene,
a foreshadow: my mother at the boarding school.
She's twelve, child of two alcoholics, vaudevillians, shadows on
    a stage.
She's overweight and sees beyond herself even then, so the girls
are mean in their pressed dresses and routinely hang my
    mother out
the window by her feet for a long time waiting for the exactly
    right cadence of *please* before they pull her back into her
    life.
That was in 1940-something—the year my mother began
the book her mind was writing called *this is what happened
    to me*—
the book she read to us—pill-language to cushion the abyss of
    two marriages—
one husband beat her up, one husband took her money and
    broke her off
with the world until she got written as *the failed suicide* after
    hanging by a thread
by a hair, by her feet, borne of her fierce suspension
over something called a *youth*.

7 Variations on Margarita Weinberg

Moisés Kaufman

Dedicated to the memory of Rebeca Clisci Akerman

1.

My grandmother was born in the Ukraine but immigrated to Venezuela before the Second World War. She told me this story:

A young Jewish woman was kidnapped by a group of Cossacks during a pogrom. They brought her into a room and held her down, deciding who would have her first.

"If you touch me I will put a curse on you," the woman said. "I am a witch." The Cossacks laughed. "I can prove it!" she shouted. "I can prove to you that I'm a witch."

Their leader smiled and said, "Very well. Prove it, then."

"I am immortal," she said, "and you cannot kill me." They laughed some more. "You cannot kill me. Not even if you shoot me. Try it."

They stopped laughing and looked at her.

"Here. Try it." She pointed to her chest. "Shoot me right here. You will see that I'm immortal." The Cossacks looked at one another but didn't move.

"Shoot me in the heart. You will see I won't die. And then you'll have your proof that I'm a witch." The leader thought for a moment, then quickly took out his pistol and shot her in the heart. The young woman fell to the floor bleeding, looked at the man who had shot her, and said, "Thank you, you imbecile."

My grandmother liked stories of heroic suicides.

2.

My grandmother wanted to be a doctor when she was young. But in the Ukraine in 1935, there were only a few seats at the university allotted to Jews, and all of them went to men. So she became a nurse.

When she told her family in 1937 that she wanted to go to Venezuela, everyone was against it. They hardly knew where Venezuela was on the map.

But her fiancé, Boris (my grandfather), had moved here two years earlier to make his fortune, and he wanted her to come join him; business was going well for him and he was worried about rumors of a war in Europe.

I don't know if it was the imminent war or the invitation of a lover in the tropics, or both, but she came here. She was twenty-two years old.

The story goes that when she arrived in Caracas, she was a woman of such delicate beauty, every immigrant wanted to marry her. (I've seen pictures, and she was stunning.) And my grandfather said, "Although I brought you here, you have no obligation to marry me. We've been apart for two years, and your feelings might have changed. You can have your pick of any man in our community."

My grandmother cried, moved by his words, and told him that yes, it was her decision. And her decision was to marry him. (Another version of the story is that their marriage had been arranged by their parents in the Ukraine, and that his asking her to *choose* to marry him was a testament to his liberal views, so she married him.)

3.

When their first child was born, my grandmother named her Margarita, which is the name of Venezuela's national flower. Margarita Weinberg. (Her Jewish name, Miriam, came from my grandmother's mother, who had died when my grandmother was two.)

My grandmother was the storyteller in the family.

In some arrangement made long before I was born, she had inherited the responsibility of keeping our narratives and our history alive for us.

"My brother was a Communist who left our village in the Ukraine and went to Paris to join the Resistance fighters against the Nazis," she said. "He became one of their best spies. A street in Paris is named after him." Two years after he joined the Resistance, he was surprised on a mission inside a German arsenal in a suburb of Paris. "When the Nazis surrounded the arsenal, he used all the weapons in it to defend himself. He killed many Nazis that day," she told us. "He saved the last bullet for himself."

Heroic suicides . . .

I grew up with these narratives.

4.

At nineteen my mother, Margarita, met a young man named Simon, who'd arrived in Venezuela after the war, from Romania. He'd survived the war by sewing and selling the yellow Stars of

David that the Jews were made to wear. He spent most of the war alternately hiding in a small room and selling Stars of David. He was eleven.

My mother's childhood in Venezuela was idyllic. The country was blessed with warm weather and kind inhabitants who were welcoming to the immigrants. The war was an ocean away, and my mother heard about it only when my grandparents would talk in hushed tones about relatives who had stayed behind and were now either in concentration camps or dead.

Simon was brought to Venezuela by his aunt, who had a successful clock shop in the center of town. She brought him to my grandmother's house to meet my mother. They went out on a few dates, and then he asked her to marry him.

She liked him, but her intuition told her she shouldn't marry him—he came from such a different life. She had never known hunger or war, except in the heroic and suicidal stories of her mother.

But my grandfather Boris said, "Do you think there's a line of men waiting for you? We are a small Jewish community here. He's a good man. You should marry him."

My grandmother heard this but said nothing. And my mother married him.

Her strongest memory of her wedding day is standing under the canopy in the synagogue thinking, "What am I doing here? This feels like suicide."

5.

Their marriage was a disaster. My mother's intuition about Simon, my father, was absolutely correct. They were from two different worlds.

My father's Eastern European upbringing, already stern and

strict, had then been further hardened by the war. He loved Spinoza, Schopenhauer, and other severe European philosophers. He was despotic and had little patience for things other than survival. His main interests were making a living, having children, and attending synagogue.

My mother loved American movies and Venezuelan balladeers and porcelain dolls. He was punctual and Germanic in his daily habits. She had the punctuality of people in the tropics and their laid-back attitude. He perceived her as spoiled and lazy. And his inability to understand her quickly turned to fury.

For her part, she often thought herself superior to him. The war had left deep scars: His manners were lacking or nonexistent; he laughed too loudly, spoke broken Spanish, and ate voraciously. (He told me he had been hungry for so long that he thought one could never have enough food to be satiated.)

6.

Every Friday night there would be a Sabbath dinner at our house. My clearest memory of those dinners was my father's bright red face and the swollen veins in his neck as he yelled accusations. "The Sabbath candles were not lit at the right time! You don't care about the Sabbath! What kind of a mother are you? This food is terrible! You don't know how to cook! The children are too loud, what have you taught them?" Each attack was louder than the last: the shouting, the insults.

And yet every time my mother tried to answer him, my grandfather would say, "Margarita, let it be. *Shoin.*" ("Enough" in Yiddish.) And he wouldn't let her respond. If my mother tried again, he would again say *"Shoin,"* and silence her.

Perhaps he thought this the best way to diffuse the argument, perhaps he himself was afraid of my father, perhaps he felt pity for him. Whatever the reason, my mother was always the one encouraged to silence. "Let him have his way," my grandfather would tell her. "Who cares?"

But the most striking thing to me, even as a young boy, was that my grandmother would watch and listen and never say a word.

Margarita was being savagely attacked by my father and silenced by my grandfather and my grandmother said nothing— not a word.

7.

I thought my grandmother was heroic. She had to be, to cross the Atlantic, to settle in a small Latin American village without knowing the language, to raise three children in this new land, and to bear the responsibility of keeping our narratives alive.

But what good are narratives if they lead to suicide?

How could she stand by and watch her daughter be assaulted and do nothing? Did she think the harassment would end? Did she not realize that my mother needed her mother to defend her?

My mother thought of suicide many times. But she had three children. That's the trouble with heroic stories . . .

My grandmother passed away seven years ago, and since then another tacit agreement has made me the writer in the family, the keeper of our stories. Members of my family come to me to ask about the past.

And so in writing this story I call my mother to make sure I've gotten it right. And I take the opportunity to ask her about these events. "Did you ever ask your mother why she didn't defend you?"

"I was an adult. I had three children. It was not for her to defend me," she tells me. "And I think you have part of the story wrong."

She tells me a different version of my grandmother's arrival in Venezuela, one she heard from her aunt.

In this version, after my grandfather left the Ukraine to come to Venezuela, my grandmother fell madly in love with a revolutionary Communist. Her father forbade the affair, and the Communist lover, brokenhearted, went to Spain to fight in the civil war. There he was killed in battle. Her father, keenly aware of the imminent war in Europe, forced my grandmother to go to Venezuela and marry my grandfather.

If this version is true, my grandmother's heroic tales served a deeper purpose than I had originally imagined. They weren't a code of conduct, or a commitment to revolt; they were simply the longings of an adolescent Ukrainian girl living in the tropics. Heroic actions that she could fantasize about but never act upon.

The real lesson she had learned from her father was: Compromise to survive.

The heroine in my grandmother's pogrom story might have survived had she compromised. Her brother would have been captured and maybe even lived a few more years had he not used the bullet on himself. But they decided against it.

These stories were the road not taken. The life not lived.

And hence she could dream them, but she could not really teach her daughter how to act on them.

Suicide was good in fiction. Not good in reality. In reality silence and obedience seemed to secure survival.

And heroism was a virtue to admire in a novel or a transatlantic journey. But not a recipe for life . . .

My mother eventually divorced my father, then married him again and divorced him again. That was ten years ago.

"I'm glad you're writing this down," she tells me. "It certainly doesn't have the flair of your grandmother stories." She smiles. "It took me a long time and many rewrites, but I finally left your father. And I'm satisfied with that outcome"—she pauses—"and that it didn't end in suicide."

1600 Elmwood Avenue

Monica Szlekovics

I remember my first trip to Elmwood Avenue. The ride from my grandmother's house always took us through Highland Park, and in the spring you could smell the lilacs as they blossomed. Highland Park was a place of great beauty, with all its flower gardens and walking trails, and although we only drove through the park, it created a euphoric atmosphere within my tiny little world as I sat peering out the car window. The euphoria passed as soon as we emerged from the park. The landscape became barren, and in the distance one solitary building reaching into the sky loomed over us.

1600 Elmwood Avenue had a circular driveway, just as many hospitals do, and from the outside you never would have guessed this was no ordinary hospital except for the eerie silence. There were no ambulances or people rushing about. The place was a fortress, with security checkpoints and locked doors. 1600 Elmwood Avenue was a psychiatric asylum.

More often than not, I was not allowed to see my mother because children were not permitted in certain areas of the hospital. However, I do remember one occasion when I saw my mother on a restricted floor, and the moments I spent with her in that room before the staff realized a child was in a restricted area have stayed with me.

The room smelled of urine and was filthy. The windows had bars on them, and the only furniture in the room was two metal tables with benches attached and bolted to the floor. What I didn't see when I walked in was my mother crouched on the floor in a corner. She saw me, though.

And when she did, she sprang to her feet in a desperate attempt to reach me, but she failed. It was then that I realized she was chained to the floor. My beautiful mother had been reduced to the status of an animal. She had bruises all over her body, and she appeared to be foaming at the mouth. Initially, I was paralyzed with fear, but hysteria soon took over and I was escorted out and taken to another wing of the hospital.

I was taken to the rehabilitation unit, which was equipped with a bowling alley for the patients. I went from one world into another in a few seconds. The patients were happy, talkative, and well groomed. A far cry from what I had seen on the floor my mother was on. It was as if I reentered the park I had exited on my way there. My childhood was marred by incidents like this, and it was from these experiences that I learned there existed a duality in the world, of good and evil. I would spend a great deal of my life entering and exiting its various facets. For I myself am now confined to an asylum that has been conspicuously disguised as a correctional institution.

The Closet

Howard Zinn

I was about twelve. I had three younger brothers, ranging from four to ten years old. It was 1934 or so. Yes, one of the worst years of the Depression. Our family was living in one of the many tenements we moved in and out of in those years, one step ahead of the landlord demanding rent. It was what was called a cold-water flat, meaning: one bedroom for the parents, one bedroom for the kids, a double bed for three kids, sleeping *zu fiesens* (head to toe, to make more room), and a folding bed for the fourth kid. No such thing as a living room or dining room— unheard of in our circles. A kitchen with a washtub for both clothes and people. A water closet with just a toilet, no sink, no tub or shower. No refrigerator (also unheard of) but an icebox, replenished with cakes of ice carried from the neighborhood ice dealer, melting into a basin underneath that sometimes overflowed in the night, causing a minor crisis. A coal stove on which we heated water when needed, and which provided the only heat for the three rooms.

Was there a closet? I don't remember, but it is relevant to this little story, because it was winter and my father was sent out by my mother (she made the decisions in the family) to buy a kind of cardboard closet that she had seen displayed in a store perhaps a dozen blocks away. My father was a waiter, now unemployed, an immigrant from Austria, who had met my mother when they were both factory workers in Manhattan. He was about five foot five, strongly built with powerful hands, a quiet and gentle man. My mother was an immigrant from Siberia, slightly shorter, full-bodied, with black hair and a beautiful oval face.

My father went out at dusk, to catch the store before it closed, and came back with the desired closet. That is, he came back with a package of cardboards that, if assembled in a certain way, would constitute a closet. There was a page of instructions, unintelligible to either my father or my mother. He set out to assemble the closet and was baffled in every attempt he made, but he kept trying, with my mother standing by, making suggestions that didn't work, and his frustration growing by the minute. This must have gone on for an hour, and we boys were standing at the door of our bedroom in our underwear, watching. My father had reached the limits of his ability and his patience, but my mother kept asking him to try just once more. So he did, failing again, terribly frustrated, and when my mother said he should bring it back to the store where he had bought it, his pent-up frustration turned into anger, and he picked up one of the cardboard pieces and brought it down on her head. It was only cardboard and couldn't injure her, but it was a terrible thing to behold, and we four boys began shouting, screaming at him, crying. Our mother was weeping, our father suddenly chastened. He picked up the pieces of the "closet" and left the house.

I was reminded of this incident many years later when I read Ann Petry's story "Like a Winding Sheet." In it, a black man who loves his wife, though they both work hard for very little, goes through a day of humiliations at work, at the hands of a white supervisor, and then in a restaurant, at the hands of a blond white waitress. He comes home, and when his wife says for him to come and eat, coaxing him with "You're nothing but a hungry old nigger," he strikes her with his fist again and again.

What does it all mean? We cannot abide by the violence one

miserable person lets loose on another. We must shout and
scream, as I and my brothers did, until it stops. At the same time,
we must think of the more profound job ahead, to change the
conditions of life that drive human beings to violence—men
against women, and indeed all violence of one frustrated, angry
person against another, one angry, aggrieved people against another.

Darkness

Betty Gale Tyson
with Jerry Capers

As a chile I thought my first name was black, my middle name
ugly, and my last name bitch. I had been called a black ugly bitch
so much I thought that was my birth-given name. If you'd
looked up the words "wounded chile" in the dictionary, there
would've been a photo of me. Betty Frances Dove. You see, life
for me was hard, and my ass was scared from the many beatins
my mother discarded. Now please don't get it twisted, some of
the beatins were well deserved, most were in today's standards
just plain ole child abuse. I am the second oldest of eight and that
meant my older sister and I had the responsibility of raising the
remaining six. Life was not easy; we were dirt-poor, living in the
slums of the ghetto. By the age of eight, I was stealing out of department stores because I was tired of wearing my fat-ass-older-
sisters' hand-me-downs. Stealing was so easy because no one
paid attention to the little black bitch walkin round the stores
robbin them blind. I continued to steal until I got caught tryin to
steal a coat for Mother on Mother's Day. I spent a few weeks in
the shelter behind that. I was raped by a family friend at the
young age of thirteen; I contracted VD as a result of that rape.
By the time I was seventeen, I was tired of the constant ass-
kickins and tired of livin in an abusive household. So I traded
off. I left my abusive mother and married my abusive husband,
Arthur Tyson. Arthur and I lived together as husband and wife
for four months. I ran from Arthur and I ran to my first trick.
After I started turning tricks, I developed a drug habit. The more
tricks I turned, the more drugs I began to use. The drugs allowed

me to forget about the abuse, forget about the loneliness, and forget about the pain.

The abuse, the loneliness, the pain, the tricks, and the drugs was nothing compared to the man who stole twenty-five years of my life. William Mahoney was the chief of police, and he framed me for a murder that I did not commit. I was handcuffed to a two-armed chair while eight detectives beat on me repeatedly. I was a trick-turner. I was a drug addict. But I was not a murderer. I tried to take my life in prison because I could not accept the fact that I had to serve twenty-five years for a murder I did not commit.

After my failed attempt at suicide, I began to realize that there was a reason God had spared my life. I accepted the fact that I had to do the time, and I began to reach out to the young girls who came into the system. I worked in the AIDS ward and I took classes in photography. When I accepted the fact that I had to do the time, I found my purpose. If it had not been for the bad choices I had made in life, I would not be here today. I would have died on the streets a long time ago. In 1998 my conviction was overturned and I was released from prison. I continue to tell my story with the hope of saving the youth of today. The choices we make today determine who we become tomorrow.

First Kiss

Mollie Doyle

I was little. Six.
Sports camp—swimming, soccer, and I can't remember what
    the third sport was.
But I know there was one.
We moved from activity to activity with tiny beads of sweat on
    our foreheads.

It was my second day.
The soccer counselor told us that we were going to play in the
    hockey rink.
It would be cooler.
There was no ice—
a cement oval with white walls scarred by black hockey pucks.

The counselor divided us into two teams.
It wasn't really soccer.
Just a pack of children chasing a ball around, screaming.
Near the end of that day's session, I fell and scraped my knee.
Blood gushed down my shin.
Everyone stopped playing.
My giant flap of skin hanging on a jagged piece of cement was
    better than a leather ball.
One boy dared a girl to touch it.

The counselor sent everyone else off to the pool and took me to
    see the nurse.
But she wasn't there.

So, he did my knee up himself—peroxide, bandages, tape—
artfully applied so that I could even bend my knee without
the tape pulling on my skin.
He told me I had played well and patted me on the back.
I thanked him and went home that afternoon and told my
mother that I loved soccer.

The next day the counselor had the group circle up and invited
me to join him in the center.
He asked how my knee was.
I told him it was fine.
He asked me how I was going to thank him for fixing it.
I said I didn't know.
He said, "Young lady, you really don't know your please-and-
thank-yous? How about a kiss?"
I told him kissing was gross.
He laughed and asked the group if they thought he deserved a
kiss.
Of course they screamed, "Yes!"
He told me to lie down.
I shook my head and told him I didn't want to.
He chuckled and gently pulled me down onto the yellow
sunburned grass so that we were lying next to each other in
the middle of the group like sardines in a can.
I rolled away.
Two kids pushed me back to him.
The counselor grabbed me, pulled my head to his, and
kissed me.
Forcing his tongue between my lips.
I gagged and squirmed. It was awful.
The kids laughed.
I wet my pants.

The counselor turned red, grabbed my arm,
pinching the triceps between his thumb and forefinger,
and dragged me to the side of the field.
He told me to go home. To get some diapers.

I ran home and told my mother that I HATED camp—
    especially soccer—
and that I couldn't even find a bathroom.

The next day I didn't want to go back, but my mom insisted,
    promising me she'd show me where the toilets were.
I did not tell her *why* I didn't like camp—especially soccer.
A piece of me was too young to trust my instinct:
to know that kissing was not part of the game.

Twenty-nine years later, I return to that field
and I play with this:

May my daughter's first kiss,
May your daughter's first kiss,
May everyone's daughter's first kiss
be anticipated and wanted.

Groceries

Abiola Abrams

Plastic? Paper. Thank you.

You/overestimated/the/groceries/you/could/carry.

You figure, as long as the bags hold out, you can leave a couple at your front door and come back for them. So you figure, so you leave two bags, jog up 3 long flights of stairs, and kick your apartment open with your sneakered foot. You mean to put your stuff in the kitchenette and run back down for the tampons, cat food, and way, way, way too many rice cakes. You are not bootylicious; it's still in to be thin.

So, you/overestimated/the/groceries/you/could/carry.

That glass bottle of apple juice did it every time. You stick the yogurt in the freezer, then you hear his voice. Smooooth, like a wannabe Sunday-night DJ.

Yo, don't worry, #6, I got it.

And suddenly your dorm number is your name and because You/overestimated/the/groceries/you/could/carry.

You run downstairs to find Bigger, the neighbor's football-playing boyfriend, stuffing fallen boxes of oatmeal and, uh-uh, tampons into your grocery bags. Luna & her revolving bedroom.

No, I got it, Bigger!

You bellow, angry at yourself for always being so paranoid.

Damn, Shorty, you must be having a hard-ass day.

You nod as Bigger swings your bags easily up past the second floor all the way to the 3rd & you gotta admit, sure does make things easier having a guy around.

Thanks, Bigger, so what do I owe you?

You say, standing between your door & Luna's door, and you take your bags . . .

Nowhere.

Bigger pushes your tampons and rice cakes and apple juice through you and shoves you into your safe space, owning it.

Bigger, what the hell're you doing?!?

Shut the fuck up.

You can't get past his blade. Your cat screams because the football player with a runny nose wrenches your head backward and slams your door closed with your nose. Your warm blood paints your face. Fist/after fist/after fist/after fist/pounds/into/your/uterus.

Stop weeping, bitch.

Which death will you choose?

Your head hits the floor, and a serrated knife snatches the skin
on your throat. Then, in a moment that seems sickly *Seinfeld,*
Bigger can't hold the knife and get your jeans-n-panties down
over your wide hips. He orders you to

Take them off.

Bigger, please don't do this. No. NO!

Slowly. Slowly. Yeah, like that.

Your legs and hands do what he says because his dagger splits
your tongue. #32 smashes the spit out of you, stomps your
thighs open & then bangs something molded and ugly into
your flesh on the crimson crochet mat his girlfriend gave you
for Kwanzaa.

You/overestimated/the/groceries/you/could/carry.

And now you're carrying much more as Bigger's dry thrusting
holds your limp body prisoner with all of the charisma that is a
knife. And my mind/won't/die.

Blueberry Hill

Christine House

Before I knew much of anything, I knew that I was defined by what was between my legs. I didn't know what it was for. I didn't know what it could do or what the men of the world seemed to want with it. But I knew they wanted it. There was never a mistake about that.

In the beginning I thought it was funny. In the beginning I was flattered. All these boys, listening to me. Laughing at my jokes. All the attention. I was the center of their circle. They flirted. I flirted. I was free to do that, and it was fun. The air was warm that late-summer night. The stars were bright and beautiful. I was giddy, if not drunk. The mood was light. I was young. I was carefree. I was out. I was on.

Then their hands were on me. They were still flirting. They were still laughing. I tried to keep the mood light. Not overreact. Not make a big deal out of nothing. But their hands were on me. I tried to laugh as I brushed them away. Just laugh. Just a joke, just having fun. But they were not laughing at the joke—they were laughing at me. I was the joke. And I was not having fun.

Then it wasn't flattering. Then it was humiliating. I realized a moment too late. The mood had shifted so suddenly. That once-warm summer air become thick and hot as their bodies encircled mine. Their hands, so many hands, were everywhere, over my jeans, over my shirt, around my waist. I was being lifted. Effortlessly lifted and carried away easily by the largest of them. Carried through the woods, away from those not part of this group. Away from anyone who might care to stop them. Carried until I was dropped without regard onto the ground.

In a small clearing. I was on my back. I could see the stars. They were still bright, still beautiful, and totally indifferent to the fact that everything else about the night had changed.

Again I was the center of the circle. This time, I did not want to be. I was not giddy. I was not drunk. I was scared. I was disappointed. I was embarrassed.

And then I was almost resigned to what I knew was going to happen. At least now it made sense—their attention, their flirting. At least now it was in a familiar context. They didn't actually like me. They only wanted to use me. This, at least, feels familiar. It's not like I hadn't had sex I didn't want to have before. It is easier not to fight. It is easier to just let it happen. It is easier, safer, and less horrible if I just convince myself that it doesn't mean anything. It is not important. If I could just pretend, inside and out, not to mind . . . I would be okay. You can't rape the willing.

But that was only a brief thought, because as I glanced around me at the huge, drunk, stupid men surrounding me, I knew: There is no surviving this. Not for me. There is no coming back from this one. I had been used before. I got over it. I was damaged already, but this. This was different. There were too many of them. They were too big. Had I really let my life get this out of control? This time I had something out there to look forward to. Plans I had made. My second year of college about to start. A semester in London. I had to go. I had to survive this. Face it. You put yourself here. This is the end of the road you chose. You were asking for it. You deserve this. Endure it. Get through it. Get over it.

But I knew. In my soul I knew that I would not get over this. I felt the regret of knowing my life would end this night. These boys, these very large, very drunk, very stupid young boys would have their way with me—discard me and move on. I would not move on. I would not get over this. My life will end here. It is like that moment when the roller coaster starts and you know there is no turning back. Whatever is to happen is out of your control, and you have no choice but to proceed.

I decided then that if my life ended in these woods, it would not be because I couldn't emotionally survive being gang-raped. That was too weak. If my life ended here in these woods, it would be because I fought to the death *not* to be gang-raped. That was a death I could live with (so to speak).

This cannot happen. Get off the roller coaster. Do whatever you need to do. Reverse the clock. Stop time. This will NOT happen. There is no other option.

Decision made. It is simple now.

I fought. Like I had never fought before. In fact, I had never fought before. I kicked. I punched. I scratched. I bit. I spat. I pulled hair. Only twice was I coordinated enough to land a strike where it really counted. In the place that drove them. But still I fought. I fought and I fought and I fought. Inside my mind there was something screaming. It was loud. So loud. Like a trapped, enraged animal. So loud. I could hear it like thunder or a train roaring through a tunnel. Loud. Blood rushing, heart pounding, mind screaming. And I fought. Arms swinging, legs kicking. And I fought. But only a few of them fought back. My terror, my frantic, lunatic-like flaying had seemed to wake the rest back to reality. One of them said something about this being disgusting and walked away. The others stayed to watch. It was dark. It was loud. I couldn't make out what they were saying. Random words. "Bitch," "slut." Original things like that.

Then someone said . . . clear as day . . . someone said, "Stop it. Just leave her alone. She isn't worth this effort."

And this was heard.

One sentence heard above all the yelling, all the noise. One sentence heard. I wasn't worth it. One sentence heard. And it was over. That was all it took. Just one of them said "Stop"— and they did. They walked away. All of them. They walked away.

One of them stopped, turned back toward me. My heart stopped with him. I thought, "Here we go again," but he walked slowly toward me, put his hand over mine, and pulled me to my feet. He helped me up. He glanced at me quickly, then at the ground, and walked away shaking his head. In the brief moment when he looked at me, I saw in his eyes something that really confused me. I saw fear.

I laughed. I laughed and I laughed and I laughed.

And that was when the pain started.

I was covered in bruises. All over my legs. Up the sides of my body. Mostly over my thighs and upper arms. I had finger-prints around my arms. My lip was cut. My hip was dislocated. Although I wouldn't know that until the next day, when the in-ability to walk would force me to go to a health clinic in town. I made up a story. I never told my mother. I never told my friends. I never told anyone. Until later . . . much later.

I never told anyone until I realized that the story was not about something horrible and shameful that had happened to me. The story was one of liberation. The story was about the moment in my life when I decided I would take control of it. It is the story of how I came to own my body. My will. My life.

My Two Selves

Patricia Bosworth

THIS IS A STORY TOLD TO ME BY MY ADOPTED DAUGHTER, MARA, WHO IS NOW A TEACHER; SHE'S ALSO A SINGLE MOTHER AND A FORMER BATTERED WOMAN.

I was once a woman split in two. I was eighteen when my boyfriend began beating me, and I created another self that floated above me like a balloon whenever I was assaulted. This other self enabled me to survive.

Recently a therapist told me what I'd done was to disassociate. This made it possible for me to cope with the abuse and also keep the abuse and the coping outside my ordinary awareness.

The beatings went on for close to ten years. We had two children, and I lived in a trancelike state much of the time—refusing to believe—to admit to the violence that was part of my everyday existence. Whenever the brutality or the pain became so huge, I'd usually escape into my other self.

Then, one morning before I went off to work, my boyfriend and I got into an argument. I don't remember whether it was because the coffee wasn't hot enough or I'd forgotten to buy him a fresh pack of cigarettes, but suddenly he threw me across the room. My head hit the kitchen wall so hard that I saw stars and tasted blood in my mouth.

Was that what finally knocked some fucking sense into my brain? Because a voice inside me—my other self—cried out, *You don't have to take this anymore! This is not your fault! You don't deserve this!*

My other self grabbed a heavy frying pan off the stove and

bashed my boyfriend's face with it. The blow stunned him; he fell onto the floor, and I picked up my pocketbook and swept my two kids into my arms (the youngest was only four months) and ran out the door and down the street and never looked back. I left everything—clothes, books, furniture, TV . . . I knew if I stayed, the violence would start all over again, and I was sick of it.

The next thing I knew, I was getting off a Greyhound bus in Newark, New Jersey. For a while I lived in a shelter with my kids, and I worked in a McDonald's and joined a battered woman's group.

In the group we told our stories over and over to one another. We had to dredge up the awful images to make the memories come alive for us. The memories were terrible—our stories were all similar—and we stopped feeling so alone.

I look at that group as the turning point in my life. I'll never forget the shock of recognition when I realized that the strength I saw in the other women who'd survived so much violence was also in me.

Today I no longer rely on the other self that floated above my head like a balloon. It's sort of merged with the whole me. I have few illusions and I do have hope. I feel fuller and more alive.

Are you surprised?

The Massacre

Marie Howe

It happens, like everything else, in time.
Someone hides in the bushes. Someone watches from the roof.
The men play with the sobbing women, tearing their dresses.
Where is the kingdom of heaven? Within that woman pushed
from man to man?
      Within each of the three or four men?
Last night watching my daughter sleep I felt my own
greater power and will rise for no reason within me:
      killing might stop time, I thought.
To be death, and not, for that moment, to fear it.
  It moved through me like a clot, clear, cold,
for an instant, I knew myself—shouting in the careening trucks
  with the rest of them—
and what, in my exhilaration, I had become.

My Mother with Her Hands as Knives

Dave Eggers

IN RESEARCHING *WHAT IS THE WHAT*, MY BOOK ABOUT THE LIFE OF VALENTINO ACHAK DENG, ONE OF THE LOST BOYS OF SUDAN, I TRAVELED WITH VALENTINO BACK TO HIS HOMETOWN OF MARIAL BAI, IN 2003. THERE WE LOCATED HIS FAMILY, WHOM VALENTINO HAD NOT SEEN IN SEVENTEEN YEARS. WHILE IN SUDAN, I INTERVIEWED MANY WOMEN WHO AS YOUNG GIRLS HAD BEEN ABDUCTED BY MILITIAMEN—THE SAME MILITIAS WHO NOW PLAGUE DARFUR—AND WHO HAD BEEN FORCED TO ACT AS SERVANTS AND CONCUBINES IN THE HOUSEHOLDS OF MILITARY OFFICERS IN THE NORTH OF SUDAN. THAT PROMPTED MORE RESEARCH INTO THE EXPERIENCES OF SUDANESE WOMEN. THE PASSAGE BELOW, WHICH WAS CUT FROM *WHAT IS THE WHAT*, IS AN ACCOUNT FROM A YOUNG WOMAN SHORTLY AFTER SHE WAS FREED. IN THIS PASSAGE, I FRAMED HER STORY AS IF SHE WERE TELLING IT TO VALENTINO WHILE THEY WERE BOTH LIVING AT KAKUMA, A REFUGEE CAMP IN NORTHWEST KENYA. BECAUSE THIS PASSAGE WAS CUT AT AN EARLY STAGE OF THE BOOK, IT'S A BIT ROUGHER THAN IT MIGHT OTHERWISE BE.

I was born in Wunrok, in southern Sudan. When my mother was young she was blessed by great fertility. She gave birth to twenty babies, and I was the sixteenth. Most are gone now.

Our father was a successful farmer. He kept 180 head of cattle and raised groundnuts, sorghum, maize, okra, and sesame. There was plenty to feed us, and he traded the rest for luxuries like mattresses and dresses. When I was very small I had a doll made in China. You know how rare something like that is, Valentino.

In 1983 the war was on and the militias, the *murahaleen,* came. I was one or two years old, so I remember none of this. The Arabs killed twenty men, including my uncle, my father's brother. They took most of my father's cattle and kidnapped three of my siblings—two brothers, five and seven, and one sister, who was eight. I don't really remember them, just as you said you do not remember your older siblings, Valentino.

There were four of us left, all under five except my brother Jok, who had escaped the murahaleen by hiding in the river. He had used a pole to breathe. I don't know where he learned to do that. When he got home from the river, my mother sent him with the walking boys, like you. She wanted him to be safe and to study in Ethiopia.

Our family moved to Panthou, where there was no SPLA. My father thought we'd be safer there; for a time we were, and my mother was blessed with more children. In 1986, the murahaleen came again, this time taking my two eldest sisters. They killed another uncle, my mother's brother, as he tried to defend the family. He threw a spear at one of the Arabs, and the Arabs cut off each of his limbs one by one, and then threw him on a fire. Everyone in the village could hear him screaming. They threw his limbs down the well, poisoning all the water for the village.

My sisters were gone and my father was furious.

My father then did something unusual. He followed the murahaleen. He took his spear and all the money we had and he went north, because he knew that very often the murahaleen didn't travel fast, because they liked to make the Dinka slaves walk.

My father spent a year in the North. He went as far as Khartoum, looking on the streets and in the peace camps for my sisters. He returned a year later, and when he did, he seemed defeated. It appeared that he had aged ten years in one. He spoke to no one. He wouldn't eat. He had been a prominent man and now he was so skinny he looked like a boy, in his body, though his face was so very old. He died two weeks after coming home.

After my father died, there were five of us left, all girls. My mother used to lament having so many girls. We couldn't defend ourselves. Panthou was raided four more times as we lived there. We worked the farm with help from boys in the town who had been orphaned. Then the Nuer raided. It was very strange, because we didn't know to fear them. But they arrived one day and they raped many of the women and took all they could carry. I hid in a hole under a tree.

In 1988 the murahaleen came again. They came straight to our home, three men on horses. They wore white and approached our mother silently. We were hidden among the livestock and they entered the hut as if they knew where we were. This is how they took my sisters and me. Five of us. They told my mother that they had been told by Bashir that all Dinka girls were to be impregnated with Muslim babies and they were doing their duty. My mother asked them if they intended to rape us there and then. The man said that no, we would be impregnated on a proper bed, and that the babies would be brought up with the civilization only Islam could provide. They tied our hands and tied us to one another and we waited in a cattle pen until the next morning, when they were to take us north. My mother came to us that night as we waited with eleven other girls. "I will come to get you girls. Just be patient. I will see you soon and bring you home."

In the morning we were walked out of the village on the main road. Most of the men had ridden ahead and we were guarded by five young men on horseback. They poked us with their swords when we walked too slowly. When we stopped to rest and for water, they insisted that we show them our genitals. They told us that we would soon be freed of the sinful parts of our genitals that made all of the Dinka licentious. Otherwise they didn't touch us, and every hour they did not touch us I thanked God.

After four days we stopped at an Arab town, and we were brought into a building that was cool and dark. It was a school. There were desks and chalkboards. We were seated on the floor and left there for half a day. We heard the activity of the town; everything seemed very normal. Sometimes an Arab boy would peek through a window at us and hold his fist up to us or spit on the window.

Men were brought into the school, escorted by one of the young Arabs who had kidnapped us. The men would confer, and twice they left with one of the girls. We didn't see them pay the kidnappers. But soon there were only fourteen of us. My sisters and I stayed close and argued over the best strategy. We had been told that the Arabs liked to split families, for fear that siblings would conspire against them, so we worried that they would see us together and guess we were related. In the end we split into two pairs.

At the end of the day there were no more visitors. We did not eat that day. We slept there, on the floor, with our heads rested on one another's thighs and stomachs. In the morning we were made to walk again. There were thirteen of us now. I don't know what happened to the youngest girl. She was taken as we slept I guess.

We walked for four hours that morning, tied together in a line, following the Arabs on their horses. It was very hot that day, and one girl was very sick, very weak. She could not walk, so she was thrown onto one of the horses and we continued. Late in the day, the Arabs began to trot their horses, to make us

go faster. I think they needed to reach a certain town by night-
fall, so the pace was now faster. After some time at this pace,
when the day was very hot and we were feeling faint, I heard a
voice. The voice said "Stop." The voice was very distant. I
turned and saw a figure running to us. It was a Dinka woman,
we could tell; her face was uncovered. "Stop!" the woman said
again and again, as she ran to us. The Arabs stopped and everyone turned around. The Dinka woman came closer. She ran like
my mother ran, with her hands very straight like knives. She ran
closer and it was her. The woman was my mother.

She had been following our trail. Our stay in that trading
town had allowed her to catch up. She yelled at the men. "Give
me these girls!" She pointed to us and she wept. "You have
taken four others. Four of my children are gone. My husband
died looking for them." The Arabs sat on their horses and said
nothing. They were very young, these men. They looked at one
another, and then one of them turned. Then they all turned and
started their horses again. We walked again, too.

She was not finished. She walked with us. She began to walk
next to my sisters and me. She said nothing; she only walked
while holding our hands, becoming part of our group. She
walked for an hour before the men realized she was still with us.
One of them turned and saw her. Then they all began to talk
loudly to one another and then to her. My mother spoke some
Arabic and she told them that she would continue to walk wherever we went. She held on to the rope that bound us all and said
that she was part of the rope now. She said she would walk as we
walked, and would always be with us, unless they killed her.

One of the men went for his sword but he was restrained.
One man, who looked like the youngest, got off his horse and
cut the rope. We were the last five on the rope. He cut it and
kicked my mother in the stomach. He got on his horse and spit

in our direction and then the group walked on without us. They were finished with us. "Fuck them!" they all said and rode off.

We ran in the other direction. My mother led us, running with her knife hands. We got off the road and ran through the grass and we slept in holes as we traveled back to the South. We ran for two more days until we saw our village again. The day we returned, it rained heavier than I have seen in many years and this was God crying with joy. He cried and cried for us, for a full day he cried while my mother danced and sang and ran around the village like she was possessed.

Dear Ama

Sharmeen Obaid-Chinoy

Dear Ama [Mother],

I sat there wearing this red and gold wedding scarf you stitched for me. Sewing up your happiness, not mine. You told me that he was tall and fair. That he was young and healthy. You promised me I would be happy. Then he arrived with his family. He wasn't my age. He was older. Much older. His beady eyes leered at my breasts. Did you not see the scars on his face? I wanted to scream, but I couldn't, for my father's dignity and my father's pride.

Bright lights. The music. Everything made me dizzy. You made me sit there and smile.

You clapped and laughed as the musicians played their drums. You didn't feel my anguish, did you? You offered food to the guests. You smiled for the photographer, and you even embraced your future son-in-law. I watched the clock as it slowly ticked away. Ticked away my freedom. No longer a daughter, just a bride.

Run! my heart said. Run. But my legs didn't have the strength. Where would I go? Village women don't run away . . . we have nowhere to hide. In any case, Bhai [brother] would find me. The village would shame me.

I don't want what happened to Naheed in the neighboring village to happen to me. I don't want the village council to decide my punishment. I don't want to be gang-raped by ten men in a hut. I can still hear Naheed's screams. "Save me!" "Please, anyone . . . help me!"

I was playing with my doll, Gudi. She was red, like the clay in our village. I loved dressing her in gold wedding outfits. That's when you signed my life away. How could anyone decide the fate of a five-year-old? Seven men, seven village elders, decided what I was to do for the rest of my life. My uncle committed the murder, and I would pay by marrying the victim's uncle. Seven men decided the fate of a five-year-old girl . . . me.

You promised your only daughter in marriage to the enemy. He is fifty-five years old, Mother.

I know how to read and write, yet I have no control over my life. I am his property now. He owns me. I will be his servant-mistress. He has waited eleven long years to take revenge, and revenge he will take. He has the right to beat me, to lock me within the four walls of his house. Even to kill me. My pleas and my wails will go unheard.

Your laughter still haunts me. Your izzat [honor] is more important to you than your daughter.

As I repeated after the village mullah [priest] "I have made myself your wife," I heard his voice: "I have accepted the marriage." And I quietly prayed for my death.

You told me that Islam gave me the right to choose my own husband, and then you took that right away from me. What rights do I have when I'm bundled off to my new owner like the cows in our fields? You lied.

They are waiting, Mother. They are waiting to take the bride to the groom's house. They are asking, "Where is the bride?"

This bride no longer wears red on her head. This bride wears white.

This procession, these drums, will take me not to the house down the street but to the graveyard by the river.

I chose freedom, Mother.

Yours,
Beti [Daughter]

Bitter Coffee

Jody Williams

THIS HAPPENED AT THE END OF THE 1980S. MY WRITING OF IT,
THEN MY READING IT BEFORE TWO THOUSAND PEOPLE IN NEW
YORK CITY AT EVE ENSLER'S "UNTIL THE VIOLENCE STOPS: NYC"
EVENT, WAS MY FIRST PUBLIC STATEMENT ABOUT THIS INCIDENT.

El Salvador. Once I come out of my burnout after eleven years of
trying to participate in their fight, the word will probably again
send shivers down my spine—it's a word that still conjures up visions of vulture spirals over garbage dumps full of mutilated
bodies. Or men and women suspended by body parts not meant
for suspension in the not so secret torture chambers of the security forces. Or priests and nuns sacrificed on the altars of death-
squad savagery to feed the rabid need of the country's elites to
maintain their own version of a divine right of kings to run their
little backwater country as they see fit to ensure their ability to
send their families shopping at will in New York or Paris or New
Orleans at the expense of others who can barely feed their
own—if you can call salt and tortillas and bitter coffee a meal.

I, too, drank of a bitter coffee. This blond-haired, blue-eyed
gringa infused with a mission to stop the killing: not another
Vietnam; not in *my* name. Fresh from white-bread country,
white-snow country, eating rice and beans and pupusas. Walking
with the poor to liberate them from years—no, centuries—no,
millennia of oppression. Intellectually engaged, analyzing the
situation, there in body if not truly in spirit. How could theirs
really ever be mine?

Flying north, home with the family, who willfully ignore my

realities because it's just too scary to think of me there. Why won't she just get a "real" job and stay home where she belongs, for God's sake? Off to L.A. to find support for this righteous cause. Now south again—semipermanent jet lag and a mildly schizophrenic haze, trying to remember which person to be in which locale.

Back in Salvador, in a little apartment-hotel, sitting by its little pool. My escape through reading broken suddenly by three young men canonballing their entrance into the pool. Now trying to ignore their press of questions of what I do, why I do it, why am I here, in Salvador, now? Best not to answer those kinds of questions asked by those kinds of young men in that kind of place—pretty clear *they* don't walk with any poor. But what's the harm in joking around a bit? Can't I escape for a while from the boredom of a Sunday when not much work can be done 'cause everyone in Salvador seems to be at church?

Okay, okay. I'll go to dinner. Just this once. You seem nice enough—sort of. And of course it is you of the three who invites me to dinner—you so clearly in charge in that pool. We dine and you talk. Amazing how much people will talk about themselves if you ask them those little one-word questions that somehow miraculously keep people spinning out more and more of their story and make it possible not to have to tell much of one's own.

You talk about yourself and what you do. Or did. You say "did." Not "do." Not anymore. Too much stress in the job. Too difficult keeping all those guns under your bed. In your bed. Always worrying if they'd come to get you in the night. It got so you sweated and trembled through the night, worrying that all those guns wouldn't be enough to protect you from the enemy. "They're everywhere, you know," you tell me, your now half-crazed eyes a blazing red. Enemies? Everywhere? Are yours the same as mine? I wonder—knowing without wanting to know that they most certainly are not.

Somehow I manage to keep it together, enduring your diatribe through that dinner from hell while I try like hell to will it to an end. You don't seem to feel or smell my fear as you drive me back to my apartment-hotel where the security guard opens the locked gates and I slip in, escaping from you to the safety of my inner room as deep inside that little hotel as an inner room could possibly be.

Take refuge in your reading, Jody. That didn't really happen. You didn't really just have dinner with the death squad. One of their own. One from those notorious death squads—they who assassinated the Archbishop, raped and murdered the four American churchwomen, to say nothing of the tens of thousands of nameless dead they've slaughtered in their frenzy of savagery. What the hell were you thinking, going to dinner with a man like that! You *knew* he wasn't on our side. Where in the hell did you put your political judgment, to make that stupid fucking decision, born of your boredom and your incipient burnout!

Tap, tap, tap.

Tap, tap, tap? Who could possibly be at my door? No one can come in here once those gates are locked. I didn't call the desk to let anyone in. Who the hell is bugging me now? I wonder as I open the door to you and those blazing red eyes. Your menace fills my room as you back me to the edge of the bed—the only place in the sparse room to sit and chat—and we "chat" as you tell me you noticed I never spoke about me and what I do here.

You spit out the words that people like me are not welcome here. And do I know I'd better be careful here? Your hot breath and hotter words sear my brain as your death-squad hands start to touch me, and the bile rises in my throat at the vile certainty of what will come next. No love in those death-squad hands. No lust in those death-squad hands, unless you count the bloodlust of threat and violence.

Do I scream out loud, or do I "just" scream inside? What difference would either scream make—except perhaps the choice of the loud scream that most likely would make your eyes blaze even more and remind you of those guns and those dead nuns. So I continue my now-practiced endurance, as I did at dinner. No refuge there, even in a roomful of people. What refuge here, alone in the room of the hotel I now know to be owned by your uncle.

Your hate penetrates me and I endure, waiting for you to exit me and leave this room in your uncle's hotel. And when you finally do, I cannot tell if it has been a minute or an eternity, but I do note that there is no smirk of the sexual conqueror on your death-squad face as you snarl your parting shot: "Watch out. I know who you are."

The door closes softly, and I force myself to pick up my book. "Read!" I command myself, forcing my eyes to move across a page I cannot really see. Keep your breathing as shallow as possible until the noxious vapors of death dissipate. That didn't really just happen. If you never talk about it, it will never be real. If you never talk about it, no one can question your political judgment. If you never talk about it, no one can ever say, "What the hell were you thinking when you made that stupid fucking decision . . ."

Untitled

Nicholas D. Kristof

It is a languid afternoon in the red-light district of Phnom Penh, Cambodia. With a male interpreter, I walk inside one brothel and sit down and begin to interview a girl named Sriy.

Sriy is thirteen and looks about eleven. She laughs like a little child one moment, teasing me for not speaking Khmer. But then she chokes up as she points to the charred remains of a brothel two doors away, where two girls were burned to death because they had been permanently chained to their beds.

Sriy breaks down when I ask her how she came to be here. Bitterly, she tells how her father died, how her mother remarried a terrible man who beat her, and how the couple became overwhelmed with medical bills and decided to sell Sriy to raise money.

Most of the venom is heaped on her stepfather, but Sriy admits that her own mother acquiesced in the sale. I ask her if she hates her mother. She fights tears as she says no. "Mom was sick and needed money," she says, adding, "I don't hate her." But she begins to play with a piece of brittle plastic on the table, breaking it with her slender fingers, violently crushing it into smaller and smaller pieces.

Sriy introduces me to her best friend, another girl in the brothel, who is fifteen. She tells me how the friend was kidnapped and sold to this brothel, but the mother searched all around Cambodia for her. Finally, a week before my visit, the mother came to this brothel and found her daughter. They had a joyful reunion, but the brothel owner refused to release the girl, for whom she had paid good money. And so the mother had to leave empty-handed.

The brothel owner, a stout middle-aged woman, is impatient with me. She trots over and urges me to take the girls to a room in back. She pulls the girls' shirts down to reveal their breasts— or, in the case of Sriy, the nipple of what will eventually become a breast if she lives long enough. "You like?" she asks in broken English.

I put the brothel owner off and order more drinks from her. She overcharges for them, so she grumbles and retreats.

In my heart, I want to buy Sriy and her friend and set them free. But journalists aren't supposed to get involved. I push the thought back deep in my mind. At dusk, I walk out of the brothel, leaving the two girls behind. I know that I have emerged with a good story that will end up on the *New York Times* front page, that I have profited from these girls, and that they will stay behind and die of AIDS. I'm just one more man who has come into the brothel and exploited Sriy, getting what he wanted and leaving her behind.

That was ten years ago this spring. Sriy and her friend are almost certainly dead by now, though they haunt me still. I failed them.

Monologue

Monologue

My House Is Wallpapered with Lies

Carol Gilligan

THIS PIECE WAS INSPIRED BY YEARS OF CONVERSATIONS WITH
ELEVEN- AND TWELVE-YEAR-OLD GIRLS, MANY DURING THE COURSE
OF AFTER-SCHOOL WRITING AND THEATER WORKSHOPS. THE TITLE
IS A DIRECT QUOTE FROM AN ELEVEN-YEAR-OLD FIFTH GRADER IN
THE CAMBRIDGE, MASSACHUSETTS, PUBLIC SCHOOL SYSTEM.

*The girl is played by three girls, eleven or twelve years old. They
should be physically different from one another, but should all
look like girls, not teenagers. When they speak, they speak directly to the audience. They do not interact with one another;
they represent different versions of one girl. When the lights
come up, they will be standing separately on the stage, each girl
in her own spot, S at stage center, A at stage right, Z at stage left.*

(*Stage dark*)
ALL: Mommy . . .
(*Silence*)
(*She shouts*)
A: Mom-mee!
Z: Mom-mee!
S: Mom-mee!
(*The lights come up on three girls standing separately on the
stage*)
A: I'm in my room.
(*Pause*)
Z: No, you come here.
(*Pause*)

S: I did ask nicely.

(*Pause*)

A: She's not going to come.

S: Maybe because she's mad at me. About that dress with the polka dots. She said—

Z: "Well, what do you think of it?"

S: And I said, "I don't like it," and she got really mad. She put it back, but then she forgets about what happens when I really give her my opinion. She says—

A: "Tell me what you really think about it."

S: And I say, "Well, you don't really want to know, because you scream at me when I say it."

A: Still, last night I told her, "Mom, I'm angry at you because whenever you and Daddy fight, you always give in."

Z: It was like there was a blizzard in her face. Then she said—

S: "Maggie, you're a child, you don't understand."

A: I hate it when grown-ups say that, because I do understand.

Z: It's mostly my brother he hits. Hearing him crying is worse than being actually hit myself. In the house we lived in until I was nine, we used to run into the woods and hide.

A: But here there's no place to hide. They call it spanking—

S: But he uses his belt.

A: That's not spanking—

S: It's beating.

(*Pause*)

Z: Mommy—I need you to come here now.

(*Pause*)

A: There's something I need to tell you.

(*Pause*)

S: She said if I want to talk to her, I should come into her bedroom. But I can't. She wants me to see it her way.

Z: Last night—

A: He hit her. I saw it.

S: They were arguing, and it was so loud I couldn't go to sleep.

A: I crept out of my bed and sat on the stairs.

Z: She said something to him, and he just hit her, flat on the cheek.

S: Then this voice burst out of me.

ALL: "Stop it."

A: They froze.

S: They didn't know I was watching.

Z: I started crying.

A: I felt like I was going to throw up.

S: "She didn't do anything," I said. And he said—

Z: "Don't ever call your mother 'she.' "

S: In school, we were talking about religion. Mrs. Rhys explained about the Church and Galileo, how he discovered that the earth moves by looking through his telescope and watching the moons of Jupiter.

A: We have a telescope, but all we can see is our moon.

Z: Then it was so funny. Mrs. Rhys was reading us the story about Noah's ark, and Matt, this boy in our class, said—

A: "Wouldn't there have been a lot of animal stuff on Noah's ark after forty days?"

Z: Everyone laughed, even Mrs. Rhys. Then I said—

S: "If we're all God's children and God loves all His children, why does God make floods and war? Why does God make people violent?"

Z: People didn't appreciate these questions. There were a bunch of them who just sat there like stones.

S: Like the day when we were talking about lying and Mrs. Rhys asked if it's ever good to tell a lie, and I said—

A: "My house is wallpapered with lies." Everyone looked away, except for my friends. You can't see someone like my dad without realizing how easily people are taken in.

(*Pause*)

Z: I'm thinking maybe I'm going to try to be a better person and not outburst so much.

S: My mom says I need to get better ways of thinking. What I like is reading and singing, because I can just sort of get lost in them and not have to think about things.

A: But when I want to think about something, I sit here on my bed, because in my room, I can concentrate.

S: If she wants to know, she can come in here.

A: But she's not coming.

S: So maybe she doesn't want to know.

Z: Me? I'm never going to forget what it's like here. How bad it is. When I'm older, I'll probably think—

S: It wasn't so bad.

A: But I'll know it's a lie.

(*Lights out*)

Maurice

Kathy Najimy

Junior high is God's little joke on teenagers. Especially a ME teenager: fat, frizzy-haired and the money my dad made on two jobs—butcher and postal sorter (with the help of welfare powdered potatoes) didn't allow for the mandatory hip junior high clothes. Although I had big thighs and hair like frayed wire, I did have a great personality . . . and when I turned sixteen, I discovered my BOOBS.

So did Maurice. Maurice . . . drove a dry cleaners van that belonged to his uncle that you can still spot cruising around San Diego to this day.

I knew somewhere inside that he didn't deserve me or the person I was soon to discover I was.

My best friend was Lavonne. Lavonne was beautiful but because she had a strict mom—and I was a "good girl," her mom would only let her hang around and go out with me. Lavonne had green eyes and long brown hair, and although she was white, it wasn't until years later that I realized Lavonne's mom named her a black girl's name. Lavonne liked me because I was fun and funnnny. We did prank phone calls till we choked from laughter . . . some fun, some really mean. We jumped into strange guys' cars on a dare, we shoplifted See's candy. We had a blast.

Lavonne and I were in the tenth grade, but because she was dating Doug (who looked like James Taylor and was older than us), one night we got invited to a party with the juniors and seniors. I ironed the shit out of my steel-wool hair and grabbed my Cost Less Imports Indian-print halter dress. Yep, my boobs were finally here, and I was gonna present them to the twelfth-grade boys! The party was at somebody's divorced mom's ugly San Diego apartment complex. We walked in (well, my boobs walked in first) chugging out of our Boone's Farm and Annie Green Springs bottles of cheap sugar wine.

It was smoky and loud. Black Sabbath's "Electric Funeral" blared. Lavonne found Doug and after a flirty batting and lowering of her repressed-girl eyes . . . they were off making out on the orange beanbag chair. Maurice De Mayo (I do not make this name up) started walking in my direction. Maurice was a popular SENIOR. He was most known for two things—his huge Jewfro and the fact that he drove around in his uncle's dry-cleaning van with DE MAYO DRY CLEANERS proudly printed on both sides. If you could see past the fro, he was kind of cute. He had large French-like features and a sexy smile. As he walked, I saw him scanning the room. Most of the cute senior and junior girls were already coupled up with guys, making out, dancing, or puking. Me and my D's were standing in the doorway; I was forcing down the wine I pretended to actually like. I guess he figured this fat tenth grader with questionable hair *might* be an option. He strutted up to me and my rack. I seriously could not believe it. This is the guy who dated Maxi—the stoner-cute, almost phantomlike *cool girl* that was WAY out of my league. Maurice and I talked for a minute. It was almost hilarious—he did that thing where he started to talk, looking in my eyes, and then finished his sentence staring at my boobs. "Let's go for a ride."

"In the VAN?" I said.

"Yep."

We got in despite the fact that I had to do an embarrassing hike up with both hands to get my short legs into the seat. I masked it with a high-pitched "WOW, this is cool" to cover the grunt that helped haul my ass into the car.

He pushed in an eight-track of Three Dog Night—"One is the loneliest number that you'll ever doooooo"—and we started driving and talking. I thought, Wow, he is actually talking *and* listening to me. Then we pulled into a driveway that led to the empty parking lot of the Kmart on El Cajon Boulevard. He had his hand on my thigh tapping out the rhythm of the song. He turned off the engine and lunged in to kiss me. I could not believe we were making out! He was smashing my mouth and jabbing his tongue in. It was weird but all I could think about was getting back to that party and telling Lavonne, "I made out with Maurice De Mayo!" He kept wet-kissing when he lifted his whole body and put it right on top of mine. He was hugging and pushing on me and groping at my breasts, which were now way free of the halter. He felt sweaty and hot and smelled like Brass Monkey. I kind of enjoyed the kissing and the boob stuff, but now his whole body was on top of mine . . . hard. I was squashed in the passenger seat—I couldn't even kiss anymore. I tried to find an empty airspace to breath. He was heavy, humping on me, and then started to lift my dress up. Then it all came to me in a flash. *This* was it. *This* was it. I was going to lose my virginity in a cleaner's van in the parking lot of Kmart to a guy whose hair was bigger than his head and who probably didn't even know my name. "Um. Stop," I said. "I don't want to do this. . . . Stop."

"No," he said.

"Stop," I said.

"IT'S TOO LATE!" he screamed at me. I will never forget that phrase. "IT'S TOO LATE!!" (I didn't know . . . was I unaware? Did boys have some physical limit that made it impossible for them to stop? Was I going to break something in his insides? . . . A muscle that, once they started humping and kissing on a slutty fat girl, they couldn't possibly stop without being paralyzed??!)

"It's too late!" He shoved his Levi'ed crotch on top of my underwear. **"No!"** I said, and in a moment of brilliant clarity, I reached over and grabbed the handle on my side of the van door. Maurice just dropped . . . fell out and smashed onto the cement parking lot floor and rolled. He didn't say a word to me the whole ride back to drop me off at the party. I reached for the van door handle . . . my savior . . . and got out. I went in, got Lavonne, a Tab and a bag of barbecue Lay's potato chips, and walked home.

(Hey, Did You Happen to See)
The Most Beautiful Girl in the World

Jyllian Gunther

It wasn't until Goldsmith Amazan punched me in the guts that I noticed his man-ness. Not until he had me backed into the corner and I had my arms blocking my chest while he laid into me did I smell him, did I see his shape, did I feel the possibility of his interest in me. We locked eyes. And it was an awkward moment because while I was laughing in the girlish way we often succumb to when it's more convenient to be treated like less than an equal, Goldsmith Amazan wanted me to forget my sex and defend myself so he could punch me harder. But suddenly, sex was all I could think of, and also, what would it be like to get naked with Goldsmith Amazan. He must've sensed this, because within moments *I* sensed the same thought grazing his mind about me. Before that, Goldsmith Amazan was just fifty dollars an hour packed in an unobserved male body that humored me by putting me in twelve-ounce gloves and training me for something where the actual applied benefit was to make my ass look good. He said he wanted me to lose seven pounds. "You're not fat," he assuaged me, "but if you lose seven pounds, you'll be better, trust me."

Say I'm not a genius, call me stupid or childish or lazy—all of those things roll off me because either they aren't true, or better, if they are, somehow I don't care if you think so. But if you're looking for my heel, the place to shoot the arrow, just tell me I'm not attractive. Tell me I'm not graceful, I'm unfeminine, discount my girl-ness, and I'm likely down for the count.

I remember, as early as junior high school, being accosted

with perverted comments from construction workers on the way to school. But the days when they said nothing were worse. I got paranoid and checked my reflection in store windows. What was wrong with me when they *didn't* catcall? They whistled even at gimps. How did a mere walk to the subway qualify as a runway competition? Why am I losing out to the crippled? And where did this derogatory tone come from??

Why do women pit themselves against one another? It's a fine line between admiration and envy. My stomach turns when I watch women scan the pages of fashion magazines, something I willfully rarely do. How their eyes dart about, taking in each detail with a yearning fused with incredible discrimination. For one, I don't want that kind of futile information in my head, but more than that, I'll admit, I don't know how to process that kind of information in any other way but to feel that somewhere inside me, *I* want to look like a cover girl. The dichotomy is mildly crippling.

An Italian cover girl. That's what my stepmother looked like. At twenty-five, she was barely old enough to have a daughter of eight, nor did she want one. She showed up the same year that my mother died, and I was grateful for *anyone* to replace her. But she made it clear she was not interested, at least not in an oaf like me. Suddenly I was an oaf? It doesn't look like that in old photos, but it's clear from my expressions in those photos that I felt like one. Especially around her, and especially when she told me so. And when I was with her, it always seemed that the world agreed.

It was a hot New York July day, the kind on which disco sweated out of open sedan windows and hung in the air like a fragrance. Add a tinge of garbage soaked in hydrant water sizzling on the pavement, tube tops, Corkys, and men in wifebeaters tippin' 40s. Summer in the seventies was dirty and sexy.

You didn't have to know what sex was to know what it felt like. I walked with my stepmother through the streets and watched men's heads turn as if she were walking topless with whipped cream on her nipples, and I felt like a ghost. The same way I used to feel when I was in the room with her and my father. The way she looked at him, the way he looked at her in response with longing. She made him want her, and she made sure he knew he'd have to earn it. How she was able to tell him in a look that if he didn't give her what she wanted, he got nothing. I wanted that power.

When we got to the corner, we stopped in front of a bodega and she went for the door, but the owner, a middle-aged Dominican man, had seen her coming and had already opened it for her. As she stepped inside, he started to sing along with the AM radio hit blaring in the background, as though it were perfectly timed for her entrance: *"Hey, did you happen to see the most beautiful girl in the world?"* She soaked it up, anybody would, it was nothing but complimentary, and I watched from the street, sure that this would never happen to me because I would never be an Italian cover girl. As if that was the highest attainable goal I could have.

Later that evening, as she was crossing the street a few feet ahead of my father and me, a bum came up out of nowhere and kicked her in the ass, then stumbled away laughing. She wanted my father to do something. I don't remember if he did, but I do remember it made me feel good, her getting kicked in her fine ass like that. So it begins.

Goldsmith Amazan has got me in the corner again, only this time, instead of punching me, he hugs me the way the fighters do when they're exhausted. Of course, this intimate embrace seems ironic because you know the fighters will pummel each other in the next moment. But Goldsmith Amazan's not planning to pummel me, and I don't think he needs a rest, he just wants, well, to feel me. Because he *is* feeling me. And it feels good. And I let myself enjoy it for those split seconds. In times like these, when a man overtly shows his attraction to me, let me admit with a modicum of shame and disappointment that part of me wishes my stepmother were there to witness it. With further self-judgment, bordering on disgust, I admit that I want her there also because I know that, former cover girl or no, she is now pushing fifty-five and her magic is half the strength of mine, me, still in my thirties. (And plus I've seen a photo and she just flat out "didn't age that well"—a concept I seem to subscribe to, despite the fact that I disagree with its guidelines, or rather, more wish I did.)

But she's not here, and that's *not* why *I'm* here, so I take advantage of Goldsmith Amazan's moment of repose to catch him off guard. In one move, I shove him off me and land a left hook to his jaw. I can feel the reverb as his head pops back, and for a moment he is disoriented. But it's a short moment, and he hits me back with a smile of approval that overlaps my girl-o-matic "Sorry!" followed by his "Don't be. That's what you were trying to do, wasn't it?"

It is in this moment I realize that hitting someone just might feel worse than being hit, that while it's been in me for years to throw a punch, landing one is not what I really want.

Conversations with My Son

Susan Miller

On the same day, in the same newspaper, this is what I read: "In war-torn Africa, young girls are very very old." Three pages later: "A village grows rich off its main export: its daughters." I rip out the articles to put in a folder thick with these clippings. A woman in India goes to the police to report a gang rape, and she is raped by the police. A Pakistani woman is punished for crimes her brother committed. UN peacekeepers in the Congo lure twelve-year-old girls with cookies and do to them what is always done to them.

I call my son. "What does this mean? You're a man. Is this something you understand?"

"Mom—"

There's a certain way he says "Mom" that means whatever I want to talk about, he doesn't.

"Chill. Not now, okay? I'm going into a meeting. I'm pulling onto the Disney lot as we speak. Wait, I'll ask the guard at the gate what he thinks. Yeah. He says he's not getting into it with me again."

"Fine."

My son has been part of this sorrowful, tortured inquiry into the nature of humanity since he was old enough to ask why it was always the women who had to take their clothes off in movies.

"Look, I'm sorry, Mom. I'm sorry this is in the world."

"Call me after the pitch. What's it about?"

"A mother and son's tortured inquiry into the sorry nature of humanity. Which I'm hoping Disney thinks is about a girl who turns into a skyscraper."

"Well, if anyone can do it—"

"Remember the mantra, Mom." He names women who have changed history. He rattles off female heads of state. And I shoot back with baseball players and their stats.

"They'll probably make me turn the girl into a boy."

"Don't let them."

I wish him luck and go on with my day. So many people seeking asylum, while I seek penance for my privilege. In the house where I grew up there was a light at the end of the hall—secure passage. I thought this was everywhere. I believed this to be like everyone's house. And so I install a light at the end of the hall where I live with my growing son.

He's seventeen. He's just gotten off the phone with a girl.

"Abby's going out with a jerk."

"A jerk in what way?"

"A jerk in the way he treats her."

"She shouldn't stay with him, then."

"That's what I told her."

"Is he hurting her?"

"Not physically. But a man acting rotten—that's not being a man."

Emily, Alison, Shoshana—these are not names in my son's little black book. These are the young women who call him, who he meets for coffee, who come to our house for Scrabble, who seek his counsel, who counsel him. These are his friends. In their company he becomes a man and what a man should be.

But there was a period of time when he did not want to look at girls or women in the context of their historical plight. He didn't care to hear my opinions on the subject, either. So I *mostly* kept quiet when he and his friends ogled the opposite sex, which had really become for them, suddenly, a sex so opposite their own that they had no choice but to study and learn it, to fall under its sway, to map it. This was, after all, a rite of passage. And I didn't want to deprive him of it. All I could do was hope he'd emerge someday from this hormonal stupor and once again recognize the opposite sex as human people from planet Earth.

He's thirty. I call him out of a deep sleep. "What is this date-rape drug? Why would a human do this to another human?"

"I don't know, Mom."

"What if you have a daughter someday?"

"Please. Why do you do this to me? I'm going back to sleep." We hang up. He calls me back.

"I'd have her followed. I'd have her phone tapped. I'd hire someone to watch over her."

Our conversation spills over to the next day.

"Just—crimes against women are different," he says. "I mean, you don't worry about your son getting date-raped. Maybe you worry about your son raping his date. Jesus. Has the world eaten up and sucked the soul out of more people, or do I just know more about it? I think men feel inferior in a lot of ways to do these things. And women pay the price. It goes way back. You know you can physically dominate, but there's an unwritten law that a man should never put his hands on a woman or child. 'Women and children first' is there for a reason. They're more important."

I'm walking. I'm walking to figure out what I'm thinking. My cell rings. "What's up with this American servicewoman putting an Iraqi prisoner on a leash?"

"But who do you think gave the orders? Who put us there in the first place?"

"Still. Mom. Still."

I miss him. I miss his face. So I fly out to visit him in L.A. We're sitting with our coffee in the morning sun, watching people buy fruit and flowers at the farmers' market. While, somewhere else, it's been another day of violence.

"How's the thing going with Disney?"

"You know, they have all these concrete barriers up around the studio? Like outside there's this acknowledgment that we're all in serious trouble. Then you go inside, and you're sitting in some executive's office trying to sell an idea, and they tell you they're only buying things that meet their mandate, which you know and they know will be completely different next week. And, anyhow, whatever it is, it's not about anything that counts. It's not about those concrete barriers and what they mean. It's like they have no concept of the actual world in there."

"But you sold it. You got the deal."

"But I'm not so happy about it."

I know what he means. I've been in those rooms, my purse bulging with small bottles of water offered to make it seem as if attention is being paid, and guest passes that allow you through the studio gates but not into a place you recognize as having any connection to the place you're from. And my son is following the same thorny path. He's a writer. He's a writer, like his mother. And although I worry about how he'll deal with rejection and compromise and even success, I can't help feeling glad he's a writer. Glad and hopeful.

The market is in full swing now. And the breeze from the ocean brings such relief, it's enough to make you feel, for a moment, that everything is fine. I can tell my son feels this, too. But he breaks the reverie. Someone had to.

"All those articles you send me that I wish you would stop sending me, well, I actually started reading them," he says. "I mean, why isn't the world in an uproar? Why are we worried about bird flu when women are being mutilated and raped? Why aren't we marching on Congress for that? And nobody has a clue why we're in Iraq, but we would know why we were in Darfur. And maybe the privileged white kids who'd go to Canada to avoid a war they don't understand might actually go to war to stop men from killing women. I'd have no problem. Well, except for food and bathrooms."

I laugh. And then I ask him how living with me, and not living with both his parents, affected his feelings about women.

"Is this a trick question?"

"Seriously."

"If you're raised by a single mother, then you know a woman is as strong as a man—stronger. I've seen mothers save their kids' lives. I think boys brought up by their mothers are closer to them. It gives you more respect for the opposite sex. And I feel an obligation to write women stronger."

I am proud of him always, but at this moment I am also sure of him.

Back in New York, the phone rings. "So, what are their names, Mom? The women in India and Darfur and Pakistan and China and here, in this country. What are their names?"

I read from my clippings. "Usha, Ye Xiang, Solange, Mukhtar."

"That's your new mantra."

As a little boy, my son imagined saving children and animals. Maybe just his imagining protected them. As a man, my son loves women for their bodies, their difference, their strength. Maybe one man's love can be an example to other men. As a writer, my son portrays women the way he sees them. Maybe what he writes will one day let them be seen.

The Perfect Marriage

Edward Albee

It was the perfect marriage, they said; *my* family said; *his* family said; *we* said; *everybody* said. And it was! We didn't rush into it; we took our time; we made sure we had about as good a chance as anybody could. All our—what do they call them?—all our "compatibilities" were where they should be—where we were happy with: temperament, intelligence, expectations . . . sex? Everything. It was the perfect marriage. And it *was*. We were really, really in love and . . . happy. . . . That's the only word.

Then . . . five years in, a long five years in, this . . . "thing" happened that threw everything out of joint. Our sex life was . . . I hate words like "wonderful" or "deeply satisfying" but it *was*. We were equals in bed, enthusiastic, passionate, under-standing. And then this thing happened and it all shifted.

One night . . . No! It was an afternoon, a Sunday afternoon, we were up in the bedroom, making love. The twins were at their grandparents'—my parents, I think—and we were relaxed and laughing, having a really good time. We were horsing around and by accident my knee caught him *right* in the jaw, bam! "Oh, I'm sorry," I laughed, and . . . and I saw a look on his face I . . . I couldn't place and he said . . . "That felt good." "No, I'm sorry," I said. "No," he said. "That felt good. I liked it. Do it again." "What?" "Do it again," he said. "Use your fist. Do it again!" "No!" I said. "Please! Please!" he begged—he actually *begged*! "Do it!" And so I did; I gave him a swipe on the jaw—nothing much. "Harder!" he said, and I didn't like his tone. "No," I said. "Yes!" he said. "Harder!" And his voice was ugly. And so I hit him with my fist and it hurt. "Ungh," he said, a groan, and then he smiled. "You made me come," he said. And he kissed me.

(*Pause.*) That was the beginning. I didn't *want* to; I *hated* it, but he was so loving and so . . . satisfied, I guess. I was making him . . . happy? The welts? The blood? Happy? Well, yes, it would seem.

But where we'd been happy together, now *he* was, and I *wasn't*. Well, making him happy had always been what I'd wanted and what I worked at—in bed, out? But I was crying a lot. We'd come to bed and he'd bring things for me to use—to try, and I would do it and it was *awful* and he got off on it—why didn't I leave?—and then . . . and then it began to change. I began to see that . . . that I wasn't hating it; that it was beginning to turn *me* on. And that moved fast and it got to where I couldn't *wait*! The cutting! The burning! The . . . hurt was what I *wanted,* was what I had become. Pain; degradation; that was . . . I was *enjoying* it! It turned *me* on! And it was so . . . compartmentalized. No one knew. No one saw anything different in us; I was careful where to hurt him; he dressed heavy at his gym and didn't shower there anymore; he . . . it was just between us; no one saw; no one knew and I'd never told anyone. And it was . . . working. The sex worked; our lives worked. It was just that . . . we'd become . . . *other* people. *I* had become other people. It seemed entirely . . . normal; it *worked.*

And then . . . and then yesterday happened. We'd had dinner with some friends. We came home; we spoke to the nanny; we said goodnight to the twins. They asked why tickling each other works but tickling themselves doesn't. "It's all about what turns you on," he said to them. "What does that mean?" they said. "Never mind," I said. We went off to our room; we got ready for bed. I put on my harness and all. I watched him undress, ran my hand over some of his scars. "Off we go," I said. "Why don't we just go to sleep," he said. "No!" I said. "I have something for you." "All right," he said—shrugging, I think. It wasn't much, a new way of doing something old—but "better." We started the routine; I started cursing and I spit at him—not at his face yet; I saved that. He was *getting* with it. And I took the little gouge I'd gotten us and I'd put it in him . . . in his, *you* know . . . and I began to turn it and . . . THAT HURT!!! He screamed at me. THAT HURT ME!!! And there was pain in it and . . . and something more . . . there was . . . *rage*! YOU HURT ME!!! And there was hatred in his eyes and . . . spit coming from his mouth. YOU HURT ME!!! And he didn't move. And then he *slapped* me— hard!! And stared at me with such . . . hatred? Maybe. I don't know. I backed off. "I'm sorry," I said and I left our room, him just staring at me, something . . . something in his eyes I didn't understand. At least I didn't *think* I did. But, maybe I did— maybe I *do*. He doesn't want the person he turned me into anymore—who he made me into wasn't . . . What does he want!? Is he through with the game? *This* game? Does he want me *out* of the leather? Out of the harness? Does he want it all back the way it was before he ripped out who I was and made me who he wanted—*what* he wanted? I can't go back to that! I . . . I . . . I don't know how! I don't know who I was!! Or . . . was that what I saw in his eyes even *more*!? Does *he* want the leather? Is *he* going to strap on the harness, and am *I* going to learn to like to hurt? To be cut? Is *that* what he's after—a complete turn around!? And am I supposed to learn to *like* this— become this?

(*Eyes far away.*) I probably *can*. I became the other. I love him so much. I love our perfect marriage so much. But . . . if I can *do* this—if I can take the burns and the whippings and the knives— if I can learn to *love* that—*become that,* then somewhere I will have passed back through who I was before it all began. I'll move past who I was when it all began. And I don't *remember* that; I don't *remember* her! I remember we were perfect. Everybody *said* so. And *we* said so. We were perfect. But . . . who *were* we? Who *was* I? Who *am* I? I can't do anything. I can't leave. I don't know who I am!

(End)

None of Us Are Monologists (aka Chill)

Anna Deavere Smith

December 1996—an expensive New York loft or apartment—a snowy night.

Gaudelieve, tall, Rwandan, Tutsi, beautiful, a model, early twenties, facing us, scantily dressed but wearing animal fur of some kind—mink, maybe, full-length, boots, long expensive earrings, huge rock on her left hand, sipping Scotch on the rocks. Accent is French and Kinyarwandan combined.

Beside her is Olivia, white, a stylist, American, Gaudelieve's age, average height, in the hippest possible clothing and hair but not "done." Perhaps a couple of piercings.

The two women face the audience the entire time and look at each other only when it is specifically stated.

OLIVIA
She's talking about what happened tonight, James.
(*Pause*)
Before you went for sushi.
After the Nan Goldin show.
It happened outside of the Whitney, on the street.

GAUDELIEVE
(*Calm*)
James. Tonight we leavin' the party, and dis big guy, he got his lady and he draggin' her on the ground—

OLIVIA
(*Calm*)
Hold on a minute, James—

GAUDELIEVE
(*On her feet, accelerating, suddenly full volume, yelling, her side of a full-fledged fight*)
What you mean—"For Chrissake, we don't haff to go over dis again, do we?" Dis don't have nothing to do wif Christ!

OLIVIA
(*Immediate—no buildup. They're there—enough to wake the neighbors, gloves are off, words are flying*)
What am I doing here at four A.M.? Who am I? Just a hack who does her makeup—not a fancy-pants. I don't belong in your fancy *lair*, is that what you mean? I used to be fancy enough to bring girls to you up here or Paris/Berlin/Milan/Saint Tropez/ wherever, before you met her, right? Oh? Oh? Oh?

GAUDELIEVE
(*Another increase in volume and intensity*)
How we gonna went "over it" already . . .

OLIVIA
(*She's loud; a barrage of words*)
Honest to God, Jesus Christ, James—she came to my place at one A.M. and asked me to come back here to talk to you— obviously she didn't feel comfortable coming back here alone to deal with you. Ever think of that? What? Snorting? Snorting what? You know damn well I'm clean! Oh, James, really? What, specifically, did she snort and when? Before she met you, she never *drank* anything stronger than porridge, goats'

milk, and Coca-Cola—'course everybody drinks Coca-Cola.
'Course.

GAUDELIEVE
(*Even louder, what a duet. Poor James*)
How we gonna "went over it already, at Nobu," James, when
everybody talking, drinkin' sake, laughing?

OLIVIA
(*In charge, outshouting them both*)
I'm just *saying*—James! The two of you saw two different things
tonight, and you need to talk about it!

GAUDELIEVE
(*Top of the fight*)
You thinks you want to marry me, but you don't know me,
James.

(*Big pause / shift / quiet now*)

GAUDELIEVE
I am talking about tonight. About what you did when the big
guy draggin' his lady on the ground! Right in front of you face.
What did you do? Anything? Outside of the musee. Her—
head—on—the—ice—on the ground! And I'm like, "James, we
gotta 'elp dis woman!"
(*Pause*)
. . . And the big guy go out into the street, and he get a taxi to
come. And he tryin' to put the lady in the taxi, but she falling
out, she keep falling out, and I'm seein' dis an' I'm like, "She
gonna broke her neck, she gonna broke her head." An' I'm
tryin' to help, and you pullin' me back, James. And all you ma-

zungos just watchin'. And the taxi driver get out and he yelling—because he—don't—want—to—have—to—wait—while the girl get in the car. (*Acting this out*)

The taxi driver screaming: "Get in the car—you fucking you mother—"

OLIVIA
Motherfucker.

GAUDELIEVE
—and the mazungos, the white guy wif de lady, he screaming back at the taxi driver, "You shut your mouth, you . . . you . . ."

OLIVIA
"Q-tip." She told me the white guy called the Muslim cabdriver a Q-tip. My *God* . . .

GAUDELIEVE
Dey bof yelling, and I'm like, to bof of dem: "Why you so raging? You got you home, you got you life, you got your, your . . . *democracy* . . .

OLIVIA
(*Under her breath*)
So-called.

GAUDELIEVE
And the big guy *hit* the taxi driver! I'm, like, '*orrified,* and James, you like, "Chill. Chill. Sssh. Ssshh." And the lady, she on the ground wif her head scraping the ground. She like—

OLIVIA
Upside down. Un-fucking-believable.

GAUDELIEVE
And the taxi driver go off fast, mad, loud. Another taxi come,
and the big guy got the woman like dis, like a sack, like a refugee
sack—and he pick her up and *push*—

OLIVIA
—shoves—

GAUDELIEVE
—her in the cab. Like a sack—a sack—a sack—
(*Pause*)
I look at all you mazungos, you white people—you all jus' looking. Jus' watching—looking—an' James, dass when you broke
the straw of the camel.

OLIVIA
James, apparently, the straw that broke the camel's back was
what you said about how "that was a nice piece of downtown
performance art"? Did you really say that, James?
(*Pause—They stare him down, not with hostility but with scrutiny
and curiosity, as if he is an object they've never seen before*)
Oh.
(*Olivia and Gaudelieve turn quickly and look at each other,
which they have not done till now, and then they face front
again*)
You were just repeating what an *art critic* in the crowd said?
(*Beat; Gaudelieve and Olivia look at each other again*)
I personally try to be careful who I quote. I mean, why give more
airtime to bullshit?

(*Beat*)

GAUDELIEVE
James—tonight make Rwanda come on my mind. Strong. About
when the Hutus, they gonna kill my youngest brother—my
mother was by his side in the road? You know dat story, right?
But you don't really know. Tonight make me think I gotta tell
you—the whole story. My mother, she put her arms out like this—
(*Stretches her arms out*)
Begging? And the Hutu soldier wif de machete said to her: "Why
is it dat you Tutsi women always putting you arms out like beg-
gars, let me help you so you don't have to do that anymore."
And he cut them. Her arms. Like he cut dem, but—*off*.

OLIVIA
(*Quietly*)
Amputated them.

GAUDELIEVE
'E emputate dem. And den dey killed my brother, and den dey
killed her. I saw it.
(*Pause*)
You know I saw dem kill my mother, but you didn't know I saw
it *dat* way. Even though we went *over* it. Before.

OLIVIA
What she's trying to tell you, James, is—

GAUDELIEVE
(*Fast*)
I am sitting here in my Tutsi looks, talking to you, in my same
looks that got my family killed, that got my father killed, that

got my mother killed—my sisters, my cousins, my aunts—these same looks that got my oldest brother hiding in a septic tank for three months, never seeing the light until the rebels came and took Kigali back.

(She sips her Scotch calmly; this could be a commercial for single-malt Scotch if the sound were turned down)

Wif de same Tutsi looks, toll and skeeny, like a Tutsi, toll and skeeny as I am, never short like a Hutu, so obviously a Tutsi—I didn't go in a septic tank. I *ran*. I went to Europe and went in a fas-shion magazine. You know this. James. But you don't know.

(Another sip of her drink)

Isn't that where you fust saw me, James? Wif dose niiiccce, expensive underwears, wif my long Tutsi legs, dey make dem look longer, in dat niiccce . . . fas-shion magazine—

OLIVIA

(Under, quick, sneaking it in so as not to interrupt)
German *Vogue.*

GAUDELIEVE

Remember, James? Dat fust time when you approach me in—the bar? Heming, Heming . . .

OLIVIA

The Hemingway bar in Paris. The dude had bars all over the damned world. Paris, Havana—

GAUDELIEVE

But you were very angry, James, at dat time—about the genocide. You told me what you had heard about Rwanda, what you had read in your papers, not much had been writ-ten. What had been writ-ten—

OLIVIA
—was like Disneyland compared to the real hell going on. But it was enough to piss you off.

GAUDELIEVE
(*Musically*)
You tol me dat a col-league in you business telled you? Told you?

OLIVIA
"In Rwanda, cars are German, watches are Swiss, and the women are Tutsi."
(*Pause*)
Un-damned-believable.

GAUDELIEVE
(*Musically, pretty*)
And you said to me, dat—night—you said, "It horrify me to hear such a thing." And Olivia, she was the one, she telled me? Told me? That you are "for real."

OLIVIA
Not just some fucked-up perverted pig who wants to put a pretty woman on a private plane and fly around the world.

GAUDELIEVE
(*Another sip*)
And Olivia seen everyfing.

OLIVIA
I've seen a lotta fucked-up perverted pigs, but I'd never say I've seen everything.

GAUDELIEVE

James, you said "Come wif me to United States, I know people at the most powerful, the most beautiful, fas-shion magazine—I hook you up. Less change de world. You and me."
(*Pause*)
But dass notreally why I leff Rwanda—to change de world wif you. It's an *idea* dass give me *hope,* but it's not—reality.
(*Pause*)
You know why I leff Rwanda? James? Why I *ran*!

OLIVIA

It still blows my mind to bits that she managed to get out. She's the shit, she really is.

GAUDELIEVE

I *ran*: to Belgium, to Milan, to Paris, with my thin Tutsi thighs, and I let them photograph my Tutsi looks for a *fas-shion magazine*? My sister, my brothers, all of dem, dey are dere, in Rwanda. They are trying to forget and to forgive—to save the country with forgiveness. But I knew I could-n't forgive. I *could-n't*!!!!

(*Gaudelieve breaks down sobbing, loud, big, dramatic. Olivia is floored—she's been here many times, but it floors her every time. Olivia does not console Gaudelieve, she just looks out at the audience, helpless*)

GAUDELIEVE

(*Stops crying, speaking louder*)
Remember, James? When we learned what happened to my sister? Right here in this room, we got the phone call. You cried too. Wif me. The Hutu women abducting, abduct—

OLIVIA
—abducted

GAUDELIEVE
—her into the Congo, when the rebels came to take back Rwanda? And—dose Hutu *women*—escaped Rwanda, and took my sister wif dem, and raped—my sister for one—more—year after the genocide was done. Dose *women*. Dey raped her two times, three times a week. (*Beat*) My looks. These are the same looks that got my sister—wif—the—two—Hutu—women who took her and they—

OLIVIA
(*Quickly*)
—yank—

GAUDELIEVE
—her dress and dey say: "let me see your nice, slim Tutsi thighs." They stick a broom—and dey rape her wif a broom—

OLIVIA
—stick.

GAUDELIEVE
You know dis, James, but you don't know.

OLIVIA
You don't. I can't. What the hell do we know?

GAUDELIEVE
I take my same—kind—of—Tutsi—thighs to France and—"Oh"—the photographer said, "Oh"—"Your thighs are the *perfect perfect* way."

OLIVIA
And you know what "perfect" means in France.

GAUDELIEVE
When—dose Hutu women took my sister, dey said, "Let us see dose nice, thin Tutsi thighs that Tutsi men and *Hutu* men are so fond of!"
What's wrong wif you face James? Why you lookin' like a boy's face? Don't you remember why dose Hutu women raped my sister?
(*Pause*)
Because dey—

OLIVIA
—crazy from jealousy.

GAUDELIEVE
Because. Hutu men. Hate Tutsis. And dey hate Tutsi women. *But—dey—lust—for—Tutsi—women.*

OLIVIA
Hate and lust rolled into one big fat. Danish. See, James, I think—

GAUDELIEVE
James! Did my Tutsi looks put me in here in dis niiice apartment wif dis nice ring? Wif dis nice coat? Wif dis nice Scotch? Is dat why I am here? Am I German?

OLIVIA
Like a car?

GAUDELIEVE
Am I Swiss?

OLIVIA
Like a watch?
(*Beat*)

GAUDELIEVE
No. I am Rwandese.
(*She breaks down sobbing again*)
(*Pause—Gaudelieve looks up. She and Olivia sit forward and listen to James's every word with fascination*)

OLIVIA
"Just post-traumatic stress"?
(*Olivia and Gaudelieve glance at each other and back at James [audience]*)

GAUDELIEVE
You always say dat, James.

OLIVIA
And by the way—what's "*just* post-traumatic stress"? (*She laughs as fully and as loudly as Gaudelieve has wept*) I mean. For real. "*Just*"?

GAUDELIEVE
James. You send me to your doctor.

OLIVIA
The shrink.

GAUDELIEVE
(*Extremely confident, clear, no emotion, together*)
What does he do? Exactly? I talk to him. He sit dere. Sometime

I sit dere. And I don't talk. He sit dere. He look down at he hands, he stretch out his legs. (*She giggles, she shrugs*) What? Whattt?

OLIVIA

When I see the pharmos he gives her? I wonder: Does the shrink see what I see? In those eyes? On that face? What I see when I do her makeup—what I see, James—'cause I have to find it, the pain? You know? Wherever it shows up and—quick—hide it. Me and her, we have to deal with the camera. Then it's Roman-coliseum time, thumbs up, thumbs down. The camera likes her, it doesn't like her. She's got the red rocks of hell emblazoned on her memory, branded on the inside of her heart, imprinted on her soul. Nobody in our business likes to see the red rocks, so I hide 'em for her. Seems to me she's in some kind of deep— existential-deep—existential—existential—we're the ones on showtime. We're the ones playing in some—skit. She's seen the red rocks of hell. Seems to me she's just trying to—to bring you where she is. Since you're planning on marryin' her.

GAUDELIEVE

I did not chill, James. I do not chill. I will not chill. James. I left Rwanda because I *cannot* chill. I will never ever chill, and I just might cry forever. James.
(*Gaudelieve looks us straight in our eyes: humbly*)
(*Blackout*)

Darfur Monologue

Winter Miller

IN DARFUR, SUDAN, MORE THAN FOUR HUNDRED THOUSAND BLACK
AFRICANS HAVE BEEN MURDERED AS THE GOVERNMENT OF SUDAN
ARMS THE ARAB JANJAWEED, OR "DEVILS ON HORSEBACK," TO
ENFORCE GENOCIDE. MORE THAN TWO MILLION DARFURIS ARE
DISPLACED IN REFUGEE CAMPS.

MOTHER TO HER NEWBORN

One day, I know already to expect it, you will lay your curly
head in my lap and ask, "Why am I not named for my father?"
And I will wrap you in beautiful lies. I will tell you my husband
was everything to me, the night sky specked with the most daz-
zling stars. I will tell you he was the desert, dusty and immense.
I will tell you his love scorched and burned like the sun. I will tell
you an army of men on horseback kicked my husband to the
ground and shot him seven times. The first was in the leg, so he
could not run. The second was in his groin, so he could not
spread his seed. The third was in his heart, so he could not love.
The fourth was in his heart, so he could not breathe. The fifth
was in his heart to hear him cry for mercy. The sixth was in his
heart to silence him. The seventh was in the middle of his forehead, for good measure.

But listen, my son, for these are words I have never spoken,
and I will never speak them again so long as I live.

Your father, all six of him, dragged me through the dust, my
head bobbing over stones. When my dress tore, just as I would,
he gripped my hair, pulling me like a fallen goat. Your father, all
six of him, threw me facedown in the dirt. As I choked sand,

your father, all six of him, cut my clothes off with a knife. One by one, all six of him entered me.

I did not make a sound.

Your father, all six of him, called me "African slave" as he spattered his seed in me. Your father, all six of him, said, "This land belongs to Arabs now, this cattle belongs to us," and slashed my right thigh with his blade. So I would remember him, your father, all six of him, said.

Alone at last, in a pool of my own blood, I looked up at the wide sky above and prayed to die. When I awoke, the village pyre had dwindled to embers.

Your relatives are nameless corpses shoved in wells. My home is a pile of black ash and a stray teapot. There is no one and nothing to go back to, there is only going forward. I will not speak to you of the past. I will teach you not to ask.

I Can Hear My Soul Cracking

Slavenka Drakulić

A DOCUMENTARY BROADCAST AT THE BEGINNING OF MAY 2005
BY THE B92 TV STATION IN SERBIA SHOWS A PARAMILITARY SER-
BIAN UNIT, SCORPIONS, FROM SERBIA PROPER (ALLEGEDLY CON-
NECTED TO THE MINISTRY OF THE INTERIOR), EXECUTING SIX
CIVILIAN MEN FROM SREBRENICA IN 1995. FOUR OF THEM WERE
UNDERAGE, THE OTHER TWO UNDER THIRTY. THE DOCUMENTARY
WAS SHOT ON A VIDEOTAPE BY THE SOLDIERS THEMSELVES AND, IT
SEEMS, USED DURING TWO YEARS FOR EDUCATIONAL PURPOSES
FOR SPECIAL UNITS BEFORE THE ORDER CAME TO DESTROY IT.
THAT EVENING, WATCHING IT ON A TELEVISION, A MOTHER RECOG-
NIZED HER SON.

*While Mother is speaking, on a big screen behind her, a short in-
sert from the same documentary of a young man being executed
is projected again and again.*

MOTHER
You ask me about my son? How I felt when I saw Azmir being
killed? My child, how can I answer that kind of question? How
can I tell you that? What words can I use to describe my pain?
You say "killed," and it seems to me that you feel nothing—how
could you? He is only a name to you. But my whole body trem-
bles when I hear it, just that one word. Azmir, my son, he was
the soul of my soul. . . .

But perhaps I should try to tell you that, for the sake of others who show remorse and have respect for my tragedy. And for
the sake of other mothers like me, I know that they are many.

That day it was only the beginning of June but already very hot. Just like that July day in Srebrenica ten years ago, I thought as I put a *dzezva* with water for a coffee on a stove. My second coffee of the day. It was late afternoon, and soon my neighbor Amra will come home from work with her young daughter, Selma. Often I envied her for having a daughter; it is such a blessing to have a female child in a time of war. But I am wrong, of course. A woman's curse is different, that's all. I was grateful that Amra was helping me. I expected that the three of us would have a supper together and watch television, as we did every evening.

Ten years passed. If Azmir had not disappeared, he would have been twenty-six now—a grown-up man, maybe even married. I still remember that he liked that dark-haired girl from his school class, though nowadays it would be difficult for them to marry. She was a Serb. I like to imagine what would happen if he were here with me. I daydream about his job—he was so good with his hands—and a new house that he would surely be able to build. I like to daydream, imagining Azmir had the power to warm me and wake me up from a cold that I felt inside. That warmth used to keep me alive. But then immediately, I feel shame, the same feeling that I have experienced so many times, shame that I am alive and he. . . . Why? Why me? If someone had asked me to trade my life for that of my son, Azmir, I gladly would have done it. Not very tall and rather thin, he looked younger than his age—no more than a boy, really! This was the reason that I believed Azmir could be spared by soldiers. How wrong I was, I thought, embittered, sitting in the kitchen that afternoon.

I slowly sipped my thick, strong coffee. See, I was convinced that I was reconciled with Azmir's death long ago. Only I didn't mention that ugly word, not even to myself. What else would keep him from coming back to me, calling me, for ten years? No way Azmir would not contact me somehow, through relatives, perhaps, he would find a way. My whole body told me that Azmir was no longer in this world, the same as his uncle, who was killed by Arkan's soldiers when he visited Bijeljina at the very beginning of the war. At least I knew about him, I was certain, I was even able to get his body (for money, of course) and bury him properly. It is important to give people a burial; one should not be buried without a name, together with others in a mass grave. Why do we all have a name? We have it in life, and we should have it in death, that's what I think. And I wanted to bury Azmir properly, if he was . . . Well.

Although I felt Azmir's end in my every muscle and bone, the truth is that I did not know for certain what had happened to him. And when. And where. It was not officially confirmed, or so I was told. In the last few years there were bones dug out, bones of thousands of men who were executed around Srebrenica. Like other women, I went to identify remnants of my son. But a watch and a few photos and a piece of shirt I was shown, together with some darkened bones, were not his—odd how thin and fragile human bones look, as if eaten by earth, I thought. I remember letting out a big sigh, not knowing if I was relieved that these remains were not Azmir's, or unhappy that I could not finally get over with the torture of living with uncertainty year after year. Thinking that his bones are shattered in the woods, that he is not buried, that some other mother—just like me—looks at someone's things with fear and then relief. I was afraid that Azmir was not only dead but also lost for me, lost forever.

So, that evening I was in the kitchen washing dishes after dinner with Amra and Selma, as usual. Just then I heard a voice from the TV in the living room saying something about Srebrenica. Ah, yet another program, I thought. I had seen a few in the years that passed, always with a knot in my throat while looking for the familiar face of Azmir and hoping that I wouldn't see it. I was tired of this, not sure that I could force myself to watch anything that had to do with Srebrenica again. Ten years is a long time when you wait. Why look at that program, what could it tell me that I already didn't know?

Yet I could not resist and went back to the living room and sat down. Amra was still there; Selma had gone back to their apartment. It was not a real film but some kind of a documentary, they said, and the picture was shaking, jumping. But I could see the Serbian soldiers in fatigue uniforms and red caps, their faces in front of the camera. They were not even hiding, so sure they were of themselves, so arrogant. . . . And then I saw a group of four prisoners, young men with their hands tied in the back. The soldiers killed them just like that. It all happened so abruptly, so quickly, that I had no time to react, to switch off the TV set or something. But when another two prisoners appeared on the screen, I averted my eyes. I was not quick enough, though . . . because from the corner of my eye, I saw a familiar figure. Instantly, I recognized my son, Azmir, his light brown hair, his hands, his shirt. He stood there for a short while with his hands tied back, bent slightly forward. Suddenly, I felt pressure in my chest, as if I were sinking into water—like when I was small and fell into a river. I gasped for air, but there was not enough. I could hear no sound, not even my heartbeat, nor could I utter a single sound. I was trapped in that water. In that room, in that picture on the screen, and there was no way out.

I knew what was coming. When Azmir turned toward the camera with a frown on his forehead so familiar to me—because he used to frown like that when he was small and frightened, just before he would start crying—I tried to close my eyes. I had seen enough.

But my own eyes betrayed me, and I stared while Azmir took a bullet and fell gently on his back.

Now it all happened very, very slowly, or it only seemed so to me, I didn't know any longer, nor did I care. I was still under the water with my lungs about to explode. Then I felt Amra shaking me gently, and I took a breath. I saw what I had seen so many times in my nightmares—but now, for the first time, I saw it to the very end. In my nightmare, there was never an end, and I would wake up wishing to know . . . the end. That evening I saw it. I know it now.

When I finally managed to close my eyes, I heard a strange sound coming from somewhere inside me. The sound of cracking, like cracking of ice in the springtime. "I can hear my soul cracking," I said to Amra. She held me tightly in her arms for a while.

That night, alone in my bed, I saw the same picture again and again. Not of Azmir's death, but of his face, looking for help that did not come.

Celia

Edwidge Danticat

INSPIRED BY A TRUE STORY.

Celia, an immigrant from Guatemala, is crossing the U. S. border in an airless container. She wakes up on the floor of the container, surrounded by a group of women who appear to be sleeping but might be dead. They are victims of human smuggling. Celia looks around and lets her eyes adjust to the semidarkness. Her breathing is labored.

CELIA
No puedo respirar. I can't breathe. My asthma's acting up and I can't breathe. Ay, *dios mio,* we're still not in Brownsville. That's where the coyotes told us we'd end up if we got into this thing. This big coffin. This container. They told us they'd help us cross the border. They said they'd find a place with no *migra* and no vigilantes. Ay, bless us, *madre del dios,* holy mother of God, it is so hot. I'm sweating like a *cerdo,* and I can't breathe. Everyone is lying so still. Are they sleeping, or are they dead? *(She shakes two of the women closest to her.)* Flaca, Mira. ¡Levantese! Wake up! *¡Todos despierta!* Everybody, wake up! *(No one wakes up.)* They won't wake up.

We come from the same village, Flaca, Mira, and my husband, Julio. I was seventeen years old when Julio and I married. He was a soldier, twelve years my senior. We'd known each other only a short time, but societal pressures—the average marriage age in my province was fifteen—encouraged the union.

The military in Guatemala is very powerful. A soldier can kill you on the spot if you do anything wrong and even if you don't. Julio came home from work drunk every night because he was trying to forget the bad things he'd done to people, burning down houses with families inside, tossing babies in the air and shooting at them. When he was so drunk he didn't even know himself, he would beat me. Sometimes he'd beat me until I lost consciousness, all the while telling me that he was only treating me the same way he was treated in the army.

"What they demand of me, I demand of you," he'd say.

He beat me like this through the birth of our son. When I was four months pregnant, he kicked me in the stomach and tried to make me have a miscarriage. Ay, it is so hot in here.

After our son was born, he kept on beating me. He once hit my face so hard that he dislocated my jaw. At times he'd drag me down the street by my hair and strike my head against a car, a window, or whatever was nearby. He'd pistol-whip me, kick me with his boots, but since he was a soldier and carried a gun, no one could intervene, not even my own relatives. And every time I filed a complaint with the police, they sent me home saying they couldn't interfere in family matters.

I escaped and moved to another part of town, but he found me and beat me and said he and his friends would kill my mother and my son if I didn't go back to him. Then he started beating me again.

I tried to commit suicide by taking a handful of pills. They only made me sluggish, so I had to flush them out of my system with water. When he found out, he laughed and said I could die if I wanted to, but I wasn't going to leave him any other way. So one day, while my son was with my mother and Julio was at work, I got on a bus with Flaca and Mira, who were headed to Mexico. Then we got into this container, this *caja* on wheels, headed for Brownsville, Texas. But ay, *dios mio,* it is so hot.

Sometimes when Julio was beating me, I used to feel like I was hot, so hot I thought I'd stop breathing. I told myself, I have to go someplace where I'll be able to breathe, where I can send for my mother and my son and the three of us can finally breathe freely. But now—ay, it's so hot—Flaca, Mira, *despierte, por favor.* Wake up, please. *Ayudeme.* Help me! (*She starts knocking on the floor of the container*) Can any one hear? ¡*Parele!* Help! Stop! Let me out! (*She breaks down and starts crying*) Please! No *puedo respirar.* I can't breathe. (*She collapses and joins the others on the floor*) I can't breathe.

They Took All of Us

Susan Minot

FOR NEARLY TWENTY YEARS THE LORD'S RESISTANCE ARMY, A
ROAMING REBEL GROUP, HAS PREYED ON THE CHILDREN OF
NORTHERN UGANDA, RAIDING THEIR VILLAGES, MURDERING THEIR
PARENTS, AND KIDNAPPING CHILDREN BETWEEN THE AGES OF EIGHT
AND EIGHTEEN TO ENSLAVE THEM AS SOLDIERS, FORCING THEM TO
FIGHT, STEAL, AND KILL. THE GIRLS ARE RAPED AND MADE TO BE
"WIVES" TO THEIR CAPTORS. THE GROUPS ARE LARGELY DISORGA-
NIZED, AND DESPITE THE BRUTALITY, THE CHILDREN OFTEN MAN-
AGE TO ESCAPE. SO FAR, NEARLY HALF OF THOSE CAPTURED, MORE
THAN FOUR THOUSAND, HAVE MANAGED TO ESCAPE. SOME ARE
EVEN CAPTURED AGAIN.

IN OCTOBER 1996 THE REBELS STORMED A CATHOLIC BOARD-
ING SCHOOL RUN BY ITALIAN NUNS IN THE NORTHERN TOWN
OF ABOKE. THEY TOOK 139 GIRLS IN THE MIDDLE OF THE
NIGHT. THEIR PETITE HEADMISTRESS, SISTER RACHELE, FOLLOWED
AFTER THEM INTO THE BUSH. THIS IS HER STORY.

The watchman George woke me in the night. He said, Sister, they
are here.

Often we heard rumors that the rebels were nearby and
would put children in houses in town, but on this day, Ugandan
Independence Day, October 9, we decided to keep the girls with
us, waiting for the soldiers stationed with us. But those soldiers
were celebrating and never showed up.

So we put the girls to bed early in the dormitory and told
them to bolt the steel door from inside.

Sister, they are here.

The gate was illuminated like daylight. The dormitory was already surrounded, with lights on in each window. We had to make the hardest decision of our lives. We said, What do we do?

We said, Let us hide. We threw off our habits and lay in the grass behind the banana garden. Across the garden we could hear banging. We prayed, Let those doors hold. We never heard one voice of our girls. We were sure they were inside.

Finally, it was quiet. We saw smoke and fire from vehicles burned in the parish next door. We came out and met some of the girls. A little one said, Sister, they took all of us. They took you? They took all of us.

Oh, the scene we saw. It was a devastation. Glass broken, sleepers, clothes. What shocked us was a hole in the wall. They'd removed a whole window and used the bars as a ladder. The girls will tell you how they tried to hide, under the beds, under the mattresses. One of the little ones was raped near the church. This we came to know afterward.

I changed my clothes. I went to the office and took some money and put it in a bag. I said, I must go. John Bosco, one of our teachers, was with me. He said, Sister, let us go die for our girls.

We started walking. By now it was seven; they were two hours ahead of us. Bosco did not know the way, but on the ground were pieces of paper—for the holiday, we'd given sweets to the girls—wrappers and Pepsi cans.

We asked villagers, Have they passed here? We reached a swamp. The water reached to here. (*Indicates her breastbone*) I kept thinking of the little ones who were not so tall. We entered the water. Because of the land mines, Bosco said, Sister, put your feet where I put mine. The Lord helped us.

One of the girls, Irene, had gotten away. When we found her, she was wearing her skirt as a blouse. Then we came to a hilly place. I was bending down to pick up an identity card, and Bosco said, Sister, they are there.

I am not good at telling distance. They were maybe three, four hundred meters ahead on a hill climbing. More than a hundred of our girls. It was one thing to follow, another to face them. Then we went down into a valley and couldn't see them; then I could. They were in two lines. As we came near, they told us to raise our hands. The guns were pointed at us and I saw their faces. They said something in Acholi I couldn't understand. The commander came forward and asked me where I had been— he meant at the school. The Lord gave me the right words. I said I hadn't been there, I had taken Sister Alba to Lira because she was sick. I said a small lie.

I said I had money if he would give me back the girls.

We don't want money, he said, but took the bag anyway. Then, Follow me, I will give you the girls. Don't worry, I am Mariano Lagira.

I was full of hope. I did not expect such a welcome. We went ahead and I saw three or four girls with some rebels. When I tried to greet them, they kept their eyes down. Mariano Lagira led me to another group of rebels.

I said, Please be so kind as to give me the girls.

He said, What are you doing?

I am praying, I said. I had a rosary.

He took out his rosary. See? he said. I pray, too.

There were children guarding us. They had guns and necklaces of bullets. The youngest ones, about ten years old, looked the hardest.

Mariano said he had to send a message to Kony, the leader of the Lord's Resistance Army. Soldiers laid down a solar panel to charge batteries for the radio signal. We waited for the sun to charge it.

At one point helicopters carrying government troops on routine surveillance came nearby. They did not know about the girls then. We were told to hide ourselves. Some put cassava branches over themselves to make us look like walking trees. Soon the helicopters flew off.

We had reached the rebels at 10:40 and it was now four o'clock. We sat for a while, drank water. There were a few houses nearby, a few women there. The commander sat on a stool, and a lady got a plastic bag for me to sit on.

I said again, Mariano, please give me the girls.

He told me I should wash. When I came back from washing, he said, There are one hundred and thirty-nine girls. I will give you—he wrote the numbers in the dirt like this—one-zero-nine. And I will keep thirty.

I knelt in front of him. Let my girls go. Keep me here.

He said, Only if Kony says yes.

Then take me to Kony, I said. I wrote a note on paper. Dear Mr Kony Please be so kind as to allow Mariano to release the girls.

He took the letter I wrote. But I don't know if Kony ever got that note.

It is difficult for me to say these things because I cannot put into words what I felt at the moment. From where I was sitting, I saw a large group of my girls. And next to them a smaller group.

He said, You go and write the names of those girls there.

I went over to the smaller group with a pen and paper.

I said, Girls, be good . . . But I didn't finish the sentence. They started crying. They understood everything. In a second I heard an order and a quick movement and suddenly the soldiers began grabbing branches and beating the girls. One soldier jumped on the back of Grace. Carolyn they slapped so hard. The girls stopped crying.

I was seeing these things.

The girls started looking at me. They then started one by one, all of them, to speak—no, not all of them—some were just looking at me. Jessica said, My two sisters died in a car accident, and my mother is sick. Another: Sister, I have asthma. Sister, I am in my period.

Mariano, I said, please.

He said, If you do like this, I give you none of them.

I couldn't write. Then Angela—she is still with them now, still in Sudan—she started writing the names. I gave my rosary to Judith, the head girl, and said, You look after them. I gave them a sweater.

I said, When we go, you must not look at us.

No, Sister, we won't.

I then had tea and biscuits with the commander. We ate. We greeted each other as great friends. He told me I could go say goodbye.

Then I started calling their names.

One of the girls said, Janet is not here. She went there.

Janet had sneaked away, trying to escape. Guess what I had to do? I told Angela, Get her. If they realize one is missing. . . . So I had to do this. Can you imagine? She was brought back. I told Janet she was maybe endangering her friends.

She said, No, Sister. I will not try to run away again.

She, too, is still in Sudan.

And then there was Charlotte. I don't forget her last words to me. Sister, are you coming back for us?

———

I am saying words like this, but the pain . . .

There must be someone somewhere who can do something.

Some of our girls have come back to us, nine. One, we have learned, died. The children who run away stay for a time in the rehabilitation centers. Go and see them. You will look and see in their eyes what they have been through. They are made to kill other children. They are made to have the rebels' babies. When I think that I footed for only a few hours and they do this for months, for years . . . When they manage to return, their hands and the soles of their feet are as hard as this table.

It is a miracle they are surviving. In a cross fire, Jacqueline got a bullet in the neck, Pamela in the nose. Jacqueline's mother has died of sorrow, and Jacqueline does not even know yet. They are just children. Can you imagine?

Rant

Woman

Tariq Ali

Woman, head covered with hijab, walks to the front of the stage.

WOMAN
So many stones have been thrown at me. I've lost count. It doesn't matter whether I wear this or not (*takes off hijab and uses it as a prop*). They carry on raping me. My own people. In the background I can hear the distant drones. The faithful are being called to prayer. And my own president, in his shiny, modern uniform on a visit to your pious and devout president, tells your media folk that I lied. He says my torment is manufactured, my suffering imagined. Why? (*Pause*) Because I'm desperate for a . . . North American passport. Preferably Canadian. My tormentors now laugh in my face. So many stones have been thrown at me. I've lost count.

And my Babylonian sisters in Baghdad and Fallujah. The violated women who stare with listless eyes at the walls of their wrecked homes. Some have seen their children die. Collateral damage. Do they also lie? Did they, too, open their legs willingly to reveal a slit where a green card could be painlessly inserted?

Our voices are weak, our pleas go unheard, but our will is strong. They tell us to stay in our caves. Live there and you will be safe. If no person can see you, then he can't harm you. It's only when you reveal yourself that you expose your person to danger. Out of sight, out of mind, out of rape. We will not live like that. However insufferable our pain, however futile the wait for the dead conscience of the "international community" to resurrect itself—was it always dead, or does it awaken only when it hears the bugle sounding the call to war?—however desperate our lives, we will not disappear. We will not cave in to those who occupy our country either in the name of a religion they exploit or on behalf of those who rule the world. Our roots go deep in every land. Without us, the world would come to an end. So many stones have been thrown at us, we've lost count.

That is why we say silence is a crime. We will not stop till we are free. We will speak the truth (*whispers*) even if we have to whisper it in every ear. I no longer smile. A hot wind has seared my lips, but I can speak and I will sing. Throw your stones. They no longer hurt me. Hurl your rocks. They no longer draw blood. I am not afraid.

I'm Thinking I've Closed My Eyes for the Last Time

Hanan al-Shaykh
(*Translated by Catherine Cobham*)

I'm thinking I've closed my eyes for the last time and put out the fires in them forever. I stretch my cramped joints and muscles, pushing the heavy weight off my chest and feeling the suffocating bonds fall away. If I could, I'd laugh aloud. Isn't it crazy that I feel at ease for the first time when I'm buried in the ground? To cut a long story short, my life was a series of battles for as long as I could remember: whenever I wanted to open the window and stick my head out, walk along the street with my face and head exposed and free, or play outside with the boys in the neighborhood, or especially when my brother's friend snatched my heart away and I went racing after it, then when he kissed me and I fell in love with him and began planning, scheming, and lying so that nobody in my family would discover that my heart had been stolen, especially my brother, who followed me wherever I went, spying on me, wishing that I'd been born a man so he wouldn't have to worry about preserving my honor for the honor of the family. Then there was the moment the boy I loved told me I was his and he was mine forever, and promised to marry me, then when we kissed and touched with mounting eagerness, our breathing unsteady with passion, and afterward when he reproached me in tears for agreeing to sleep with him, and I cried and pleaded with him, saying I'd agreed because I loved him, and because I loved him, I'd agreed. He cried louder, then ran off and never came back, and I wept and wailed and beat my chest because he'd left me, and because I was scared my brother would find out what had happened. Then, finally, my prayers were answered and my life was taken from me.

I'm thinking I've closed my eyes for the last time. I stretch my cramped joints and muscles, pushing the heavy weight off my chest and feeling the suffocating bonds fall away. If I could, I'd laugh aloud to hear myself repeat silently: "Isn't it crazy that I feel at ease because I'm buried in my grave?"

But all at once, I find myself twitching violently again. The calm feeling abandons me, and it isn't because of the maggots: They wouldn't know I was dead until they began gnawing into me. My death is still fresh. I haven't gone to hell yet, to dangle from a *zaqqum* tree while burning coals tear my flesh to shreds. Nor have I turned into a rose to be plucked by an unknown hand, nor a bird to be pelted with stones, nor a ravening wolf. I haven't been reincarnated as a newborn baby, to live again inside her. No. Nothing like this has happened. Instead, darkness is falling now, the graveyard empties of visitors, the graveyard attendant comes across to my grave, digs it up at an amazing speed, lifts me out, or rather pulls me violently, carries me into his little room, and throws me down on the bed. He unwraps my white shroud, tears it off me, then rides me like a horse, his hands between my breasts as if they are the saddle. Then he leaves me suddenly, not because I'm cold as ice, but to take off his trousers and underpants before remounting me, moaning and sighing. He stops, or should I say freezes, only when there's a loud knocking on the door, then someone kicks it so hard it caves in and comes crashing down onto the floor, and my brother is standing there, his mouth open wide. He's come back to the graveyard, looking for the attendant to help him find his mobile phone, which he's certain fell out of his pocket into my grave as he lowered me in unaided, to make sure—even though I was dead—that no other man would touch me, not even a man of religion.

I Can't Wait

James Lecesne

If I had my choice, I'd have to say that I prefer being beat up to being a dead person. Being a dead person is so boring. You just lie there. Sometimes for hours. You are not a priority. They get to you when they get to you. Unless, of course, you have a major role. I've never had a major role. Not yet, anyway. In fact, I seem to be getting a reputation for being a random dead person. I've been dead on three different TV shows, including *Six Feet Under*. My agent told me that the producers have been very impressed by how long I'm able to hold my breath, how still I can be while the principals discuss the details of my death or whatever, and how I never complain even when I have to lie, scantily clad, on the pavement. I've played a dead prostitute a number of times. You'd be surprised how many dead prostitutes there are in my business. I did once play a living prostitute on an ongoing cable TV series, but I was strictly background, I was what they call "atmosphere." I wore uncomfortable shoes, as prostitutes do, and I was filmed leaning against a well-lit wall the whole time. I decided that my name was Sharon Lefferty and I hadn't come to prostitution easily; it had been a difficult decision for me because I was basically a good girl who got desperate and needed the money. I didn't enjoy the sex, and I wasn't into drugs, but I did have a weakness for really nice clothes. It was how I justified my life as a sex worker. I told the wardrobe people about this aspect of my backstory; I thought it would help them be more creative with my costuming, more specific, and perhaps get me better shoes. But the head wardrobe woman handed me a vinyl skirt and a pair of Payless boots and said, "Yeah, well, think of me as your pimp who's got other ideas about your look." That's the thing when you don't have a speaking part: You really don't have a voice in the development of your character. I couldn't tell the wardrobe woman that Sharon Lefferty was not the type of girl who would ever be involved with a pimp. And even if she had been, she certainly wouldn't have gone with a lady pimp.

Of course, nobody gets into this business to always be a non-speaking prostitute, dead, or beat up, or whatever, but that's a lot of what's out there. You take what you can get. But like I said, being beat up is way better. You get rehearsal time, you get to work with the other actors, sometimes there's a choreographer if the fight is supposed to be really fierce.

It's not as easy as it looks to get knocked against a wall. You have to know how to do it so you don't get hurt. And falling down takes practice. There are little tricks you learn so you don't take the fall hard and scrape your elbows or your knees. You also have to watch that you don't totally wreck your outfit, or the wardrobe people give you a hard time and take the cost of your costume out of your paycheck. One trick I've learned is that you always want to know where you are in the frame. Is your fall going to be actually seen, or are you out of frame when you go down? Usually, the camera stays with the principal actor, getting his reaction when I go down. I mean, he's getting the big money. Anyway, I always ask, because what's the point of going for realness and risking a hurt shoulder or torn stockings when you are out of frame and it's all about him?

There are now entire TV stations (cable, but still) devoted to women and women's programming. They are not afraid to take on women's issues and also to provide leading roles for women to play. I remember the first time I saw a made-for-TV movie on one of these stations back in '97, and I instantly thought, I could play the hell out of that cheerleader. I think it was what made me decide to be an actress and wholeheartedly pursue my goals. The movie was about a high school romance that quickly turned to disaster when the all-star jock proved to be a psychotic jerk who used violence to control his girlfriend. I couldn't believe my eyes when I saw Fred Savage (known for playing the kid in *The Wonder Years*) portray an evil bully. He was amazing. So scary. The name of the movie is *No One Would Tell,* and the girlfriend is played by Candace Cameron of TV's *Full House* fame.

Sometimes when I'm on set waiting while a shot is set up, I speak to my fellow actors. I often mention *No One Would Tell* as an early influence on my work. Usually, I am reminded by whomever I am speaking to that actors like Fred and Candace were probably cast in that movie because they both had been child stars, they had name recognition, not to mention connections. As a kind of joke, I remind whomever that it is way too late for me to become a child star. But then, on a more serious note, I tell them that I am trying to get my name recognized by being an occasional dead person and make connections through my roles as a nonspeaking prostitute who gets roughed up. It's just a matter of being patient, I tell them.

It's hard not to get discouraged in a business like mine. Especially when I turn on the TV and see Nicollette Sheridan playing a woman who has just received eye transplants to restore her vision and is acting up a storm while being bombarded with images of the last moment of her donor's life (*Deadly Visions,* 2004), or see Jamie Luner, of *Melrose Place* fame, playing a blind lawyer who gets raped by a guy who then escapes from jail vowing to kill her (*Blind Injustice,* 2005). When that happens, I get totally down in the dumps about the state of my career, and

I have to face the fact that I might not be getting the breaks because basically, I'm nobody. But I'm not giving up. I'm going to keep going.

What I'm really hoping for is a plum part as a forensic investigator on an ongoing series for network TV. That's my dream. But I don't want to be just the kind of forensic investigator who wears a lab coat and glasses and puzzles over a corpse laid out in an antiseptic environment. I want to be the kind who gets to wear low-cut blouses that are tailored to the body, flank-hugging slacks, and tousled hair while she investigates a dead body at the scene of the crime. Instead of being the dead body at the scene of the crime, or the nameless corpse with a tag on my toe, I want at the very least to portray complex human emotions on-screen and have my own trailer. This business is full of opportunities for an actress who knows how to play the hell out of a living person with a speaking part. I know they're out there for me to sink my teeth into. I can't wait.

In Memory of Imette

Periel Aschenbrand

For as badass as I am—or like to think I am—in the back of my mind, I am always wholly aware of the fact that at any moment I could be raped.

The fact that I'm totally paranoid doesn't detract from the other fact, which is that *this is true*.

So when someone picked up NYU student Imette St. Guillen and sodomized and raped her repeatedly and bound her hands behind her back and shoved a tube sock down her throat and wrapped her face in packing tape and lopped off her long black hair and sliced up her genital area before he dumped her by the side of the Belt Parkway, it didn't escape me for one second that she just as easily could have been me.

To begin with, the bar she was last seen alive in is around the corner from my house.

And that's just to begin with.

For the first few days, I locked myself in my apartment. It got to the point where I was afraid to take a shower. And this isn't some bogeyman fantasy. I've read nearly every FBI criminal profile book and every Ann Rule book that has ever been written. Ignorant people who adore me tried to tell me I was overreacting, but it was useless. I *know* what the fuck I'm talking about.

I said from the get-go that the person who did this to Imette was a serial killer, and everyone was like, Periel, really, get a grip.

So I did.

I went to the John Jovino gun shop, also down the street from my house, and bought mace and a Screecher, which looks like a baby fire extinguisher but makes a really loud noise, and a big-ass hunting knife with which, if need be, I could slice off some-one's testicles. I tried to buy a stun gun, but the Chinese person behind the counter said, "Po-rees only."

I was unhappy about that because I thought the gun, in addi-tion to being able to immobilize someone, would be a fairly sexy accessory. I made do, and for about two weeks, I walked around with my hands in my pockets, the Screecher in one hand and the mace in the other. I was petrified. I was also ready to seriously fuck someone up.

When I profiled the killer over dinner, I explained that some-one who commits a crime like this has raped before because it was a fairly organized crime. It's clear by the *way* he killed her that he enjoyed it and that he would not be someone who could be rehabilitated—based on the fact that it was so violent, he'd likely been fantasizing about something like this for years. My friend looked at me and said, deadpan, Wow, P. It sounds like you're about to crack this case wide open.

I was like, You can make fun of me if you want, but you'll see. When they find this guy, he'll have raped and killed before. And if they don't catch him, he'll *definitely* do it again. This guy *gets off* on this. Don't you get it? He likes this. It's a game to him. He enjoys the torture. And I'm not going down! I screamed as I exhibited my array of weaponry.

My friend continued to look at me as though I had com-pletely lost my mind.

I continued: Imette St. Guillen was a student of forensic psy-chology. If *anyone* knew about these sociopaths, it was her. Two of her fingernails were ripped off. Do you know what that means? She fought like a fucking tiger. It means if this happened to her, it could happen to anyone. Don't you get that?

But wait, you're a guy. You have nothing to worry about. Se-rial killers almost never kill grown men.

So there you fucking go. With your six feet of height and your dick between your legs, you have nothing to worry about. Except for me. You should be worried about me. You should be very worried about me, because the reality is that, literally at any point, I could be raped.

This is a fact that is lost on most men. Not because they don't love us but more because they just don't understand what it feels like to walk down a dark street and see a creepy guy and be scared for your life. They don't understand because they can't understand.

So for Imette and for all the other women who have met their fate in a fashion so hideous most of us don't dare to even think of it, I'm thinking of you, and though I'm bathing again, I'm still carrying a knife in my back pocket.

Respect

Kimberle Crenshaw

Black vaginas
the hardest-working vaginas in America,
and still they get no respect.
No vagina has done so much for this country
and received so little. Really.
Black vaginas built this country.
It all started right here,
between blueberry black, chocolate cream, honey brown,
praline pecan
French vanilla
legs.
It wasn't the Declaration of Independence,
the Constitution,
or the Stars and Stripes that gave birth to America.
It was the black vagina that laid the golden egg,
or rather, the chattel slave.
That's right—during America's formative years, the most
     valuable property it produced,
the property that the entire economy was based on,
the property that was mortgaged to build America
was property in slaves.
Twelve billion dollars' worth.
One can't begin to fathom it in today's dollars. And where did
     it come from? Whose vaginas passed this twelve billion
     dollars?
Whose vaginas were capitalized, colonized, and amortized all
     to give birth to America?

Whose vaginas have been appropriated, syndicated, deprecated,
    but never, ever
vindicated in the process of building this country?
The black vagina, the only vagina that was less valuable when
    it was protected, loved, and respected
than when it was open, taken, and occupied at will.
And the law made it that way—black women couldn't be raped
    as a matter of law during those old days.
The law said
that rape was something that happened to white vaginas,
not to black ones.

But those were the old days, we can rest assured.
We finally got that Respect that Aretha's been talking about all
    these years.
Or did we?
Has the black vagina received the respect she deserves even
    today?
Is it respected when those who enter our vaginas against our
will are least likely to be arrested, least likely to be prosecuted,
least likely to be convicted, and when, by some miracle, they
are convicted, they will receive only one-fifth the sentence of
those who rape white vaginas?

Is it respected when no one seems to know or care about what
happens to our vaginas within our community, right here in
Harlem?

Is it respected when everyone knows about the Central Park
Jogger, but no one knows about the eight other women of color
raped in New York that very week, one who was gang-raped,
thrown down an elevator shaft, and left for dead?

Is the black vagina respected when our own community readily embraces those accused of rape, and chastises a woman for "not having the good sense God gave her" or "having no business being up there with that man at two in the morning" or "being foolish not to know what the brother's true intentions were"?

Is it respected when politicians trip over themselves trying to be tough on black vaginas by embracing punitive policies to sew up and shut down these vaginas now that our labor isn't needed anymore?

After four hundred years, is *this* the *respect* we've been waiting for?
I don't think so . . .

So here's an idea. The next time we hear ReRe belting out R>E>S>P>E>C>T,
let's reach for it, own it, proclaim it as our national anthem for
    black vaginas,
for all vaginas,
because we know that respect goes to those
who demand it, expect it, and refuse to live without it
So from Harlem to Watts
from Memphis to Detroit
from Nairobi to Beijing
from Kingston to Jerusalem
let our voice, our demand, our command, be heard:
RESPECT this vagina!!!

The Aristocrats

Kate Clinton

I sobbed through the movie *The Aristocrats*.

To clarify, *The Aristocrats* is not a documentary about the Bushes.

The Aristocrats is a movie about the world's filthiest joke and the comics who love to tell it. Here's how it goes: A showbiz family visits a vaudeville talent agency. The agent asks the father to describe their act. The father proceeds: The family dog is trained to poop in their son's mouth while the boy is copulating with their nine-year-old daughter while the father is urinating on the mother, and on and on. The agent asks the father what they call themselves. The father says, "The Aristocrats."

Hi-larious.

By process of natural selection, the fittest survivors of the film's comic Darwinism, the aristocrati of comedy, are mostly male. The comic elders mouth the classic line, which I heard often in my career, "Look, funny is funny." That gender erasure reminds me of something June Jordan once said: "There is power and there is point of view and whoever has the power determines the point of view."

So, the ejaculatory stand-up/punch-line brand of male humor has a funny point of view, while the multiorgasmic, extended storytelling of women does not have a funny point of view. Because the long multipart middle section of the Aristocrats joke is safely bracketed by the familiar levees of setup and punch line, when men tell it, it is hilarious.

But I was sobbing.

Men have always said that women have no sense of humor.

Often after we've been seen together laughing, howling, tears streaming down our faces. Men can feel so left out. It's just that women know whose butts are the butts of the jokes.

I grew up in a land of reversals. Where men who told jokes about women were funny but women who told jokes about men were anti-male. Where, year after year, there was the appearance of a cartoon depicting the same "funny" scene of a barelegged man in an old raincoat exposing himself to a woman. The cartoon was made even "funnier" by the horrified look on the woman's face. By extension, rape was one of the funniest things a guy could do. The ultimately practical joke.

I remain a faith-based comedian. I believe in the power of laughter in a democracy. It takes the tyranny of the things we are given, and it blows them apart. When I'm listening to someone tell me the largest pile of crap, I nod, listen, and then just burst out laughing. I pause, then say, Oh my God, you mean it. And that person will never say those things again with any degree of confidence. And it's time to take them down.

God told me. She did.

Connect: A Web of Words

Robin Morgan

• Threat • Shout • Bellow • Hit • Slap • Smack • Strike • Beat • Bash • Batter • Pummel • Punch • Slash • Stamp • Pound • Maul • Hammer • Bludgeon • Fist • Belt • Knife • Gun • Punish • Control • Mutilate • *Blood* • Ambulance • Sorry • Drunk • Welt • Swollen • Scar • *Lies* • Made Me Do It • Deserved It • Her Own Fault • Taught a Lesson • *Shame* • Neighbors • Secret • Whimper • *Fear* • Skulk • Shuffle • Wince • Tremble • Shudder • Shake • Cower • Cringe • Flinch • Crawl • Listen • Wait • Whisper • Bruise • Bandage • *Guilt* • Bumped into a Door • He Didn't Mean • Shatter • Wound • Fracture • Rupture • Harassment • Provoked It • Stalking • Invited It • Restraining Order • Funeral • *Scream* • Stranger Rape • Acquaintance Rape • Date Rape • Marital Rape • Child Rape • Asked for It • Wanted It • *Entitlement* • Masculine • *Selflessness* • Feminine • Disgust • Bitch • Cunt • Slit • 'Ho • Witch • Hag • Illiteracy • Purdah • Suttee • Clitoridectomy • Infibulation • Stoning • *Terror* • Burka • Chador • Forced Shrouding • Pornography • Forced Exposure • Sex Traffick • *Hunger* • Child Bride • Kidnapped Bride • Mail-order Bride • Bride Burnings • Harem • Forced Marriage • Child Marriage • Slavery • *Humiliation* • Tears • Begging • Prostitution • *Poverty* • Hooker • Pimp • John • Brothel • *Loneliness* • Hemorrhage • *Lovelessness* • Dread • *Exhaustion* • Hide • Run • Where • Duty • Family • Minister • Priest • Rabbi • Mullah • Trapped • *Again* • Stupid • Ugly • Fat • Old • Face-lift • Backstreet Abortion • Maternal Mortality • Female Infanticide • Suicide • *No* • Femicide • Gynocide • Genocide • Silence • *No* • Weep • Howl • *Blood* • Gasp • Wail • Grief • Mourning • Secrets • Lies • Propaganda

• Torture • Waterboard • Electrodes • Lash • Cane • Whip • Burn • *Starve* • Boy Next Door • Serial Killer • Gang • Sect • Nation • Empire • Molotov Cocktail • IED • Patriot Missile • Peacekeeper Missile • "Big Boy" A-bomb • "Nuclear Hardness" • "Deep Penetration Capacity Bomb" • "Potent Kill Capability" • "Rigid, Hardened Silo" • "Erector Launchers" • "Thrust Ratios" • "Soft Targets" • Toy Gun • Toy Tank • Toy Missile • *No* • How • *Planet* • *Why* • Madness • *Rage* • Shrill • Strident • *Yes* • Crazy • *Hope* • Bread • Shelter • You *Too?* • Recognition • *Truth* • Strength • Dignity • Yes • *Transformation* • Human • *Together* • Yes •

Stew

Ariel Dorfman

"Your husband is still alive."

It was not familiar, the rasping voice of that man, not familiar at all, no matter how much I searched for something, anything, that would let me trust him, believe what the stranger on the other side of the phone was saying, that he really knew my husband was not dead. Proof, I wanted proof, wanted to ask where, when, how, friend, foe, near, far.

Instead, serenely:

"Bless you, if what you say is true."

"Of course it's true. Last night, I saw your husband just last night. We shared a cell together, he asked me to call you, gave me your name."

But I still didn't dare say what I really wanted to say. Behind me, the children began to cry. Why did they begin to cry just then? Were they warning me to be careful? Were they catching something from the strangled breathless language of my body as I held the phone too close to my ear, the slim slope of my body that he loved to touch and slender downwards with his hands, my man, my man, my body now so abruptly rigid that it scared the children? Or were they crying because they were hungry, set off by the smallest one, she who has never seen her father, who does not even know there is such a thing as a father, hungry for my milk as I stifled my words into the phone, hungry for the hands of a father to soothe her when there is no milk, when the lights sputter off in the night and the bombs fall nearby and my breasts grow sour.

"He is well, you are telling me that my husband is well?"

And the response was what I expected and is not, can never be, what I expect, the response from that rasp, that voice that has coughed too much, perhaps from too many cigarettes, perhaps, perhaps from too many screams wrenched from that throat: "Nobody can be said to be well in that place, that wet hole out of hell—that place is so dark, so dark I don't even know what your husband's face looks like, what he is wearing, I could not describe him to you if you asked—but do not ask, do not ask. Be glad he is alive and do not ask anything else."

"All I'm asking is that he come home." And then I add, so this man on the phone doesn't get any wrong ideas, heading off this man and his rasp, just in case, just in case this time this one also has plans, I blurt out: "We need him so much, my husband. Since they came for him, we haven't had any income, not a penny, only a package every week from his old mother—" I stress that word, **old**. That word, **mother**. Draw both words out, accentuate them, see if that moves this one, the man on the other side of the line, moves him to pity, to understand that we are like orphans, we have nothing to tender, nothing that he can squeeze out of us, out of me—

Have I made a mistake? Did I speak too soon of what we lack, of our destitution, am I frightening him away?

Because now the man interrupts me.

"I'm in a hurry," the man says, suddenly impatient, and there is a coldness in his voice that was not there before. As if he resents my implication that he expects recompense, as if he is angry that I am poisoning his act of kindness. "I can't talk much longer. They said if I called anyone, if I told anyone about this, anything, they would come for me again. We know you, we know where you live, we know where your brother lives, your mother, my mother is also old. So I will call you again soon. Goodbye."

Now I don't lose a second wondering what to say. Now I whisper out urgently:

"Wait, wait—"

Just that, wait, wait.

And he manages to shred out a few more words, grind them into my ears:

"I will tell you more next time," that is what he says.

"Wait, wait!"

And then the phone goes dead before I can add: "Tell me where he is, how to get him out, why they took him, I will do anything to bring him back alive."

I will do anything, anything, to bring him back alive.

What I said to the other one, the other time, the last time, when the phone rang two months ago and another voice, without a rasp, that voice, like honey, that voice saying my husband was alive, still alive. And then added **I will tell you more later,** asked for money, asked me to bring the money to the corner of that street and **also some of that stew you fix, your husband says you cook great stew, woman,** and how to recognize him, **you'll recognize me, I will be smoking and I am a big man, a large man, you won't have any trouble recognizing me.** And two days and ten hours later, I watched him, that other man back then, count the bills under the streetlamp, lick his thumb each time to make sure he had not missed a bill and then, **it is not enough,** he said, as I knew he would, **not enough, if I am to risk my life getting your husband free, bribing the guards, I will need more, much more than this.** And then he tasted the stew, I saw his fingers go into the pot and come out with a chunk of meat and **oh yes, oh yes, this is as good as I was told, but still, still not enough.** And He knew, that man under the big hulk of his shoulders, those delicate bones of his holding up the enormous weight of his flesh, he knew and I knew that this was not the end of it. I had

told him that I would do anything, anything, to bring the father
of my children back alive, I had made that mistake. I knew, even
when we parted later that night and he swore he would call
again with his voice still like honey, I knew I would never hear
from him again.

And now? What now?

Now, two months later, I wait with the phone in my hand and
behind me the children, all three of them quiet, and it is worse
than when they cried, and the dead buzz of the dead phone is
more familiar than the voice that just said goodbye, I already
miss the recent rasp of that voice, the flash of a promise in his
throat that may have screamed too much in the dark, **I will tell
you more, I'll call you again.** Did he say that? **I will call you
again?**

What if he's dialing my number right now? Forgot one last
thing? Is ready to provide proof that my husband is really still
alive? What if the other one, the man with the honey voice and
the big hands under the streetlamp, is dialing my number right
now?

But I don't let the phone go. As soon as I let the phone coil
and snarl back to where it was before this latest call, I know that
as soon as I force the receiver back into its cradle, that's it, that
will be it, there will be nothing to do with my body except sit
here, park my body here, and then it will be dawn and then another day and then the next week and the month after that, waiting, waiting, waiting for the next call, this man of the rasp or
that man of the voice like honey or another man, another man
with whatever voice his mother offered him as a gift the moon-
less night he was born, someone, anyone with news, anyone to
ask if my husband is still wearing the same shirt he was wearing
the day they took him, did they uncover his head soon, don't
they realize he's asthmatic, can't breathe well under that rough

dark bag they tied around his beautiful face, hid away his beautiful curly hair, someone to ask who sews his buttons, is he hungry, is he hungry for the meat I will prepare for him when he comes back, succulent and juicy and slightly sweet, does he know the child was a girl, does he know he has a daughter, someone, anyone to ask, anyone to say yes to, yes, yes, I will do anything, anything, anything to bring back alive the love of my life.

Anything, anything.

The phone is still in my hand and the baby has started to cry.

I put the receiver back, I put the receiver back again and wait for the next call.

The Next Fantastic Leap

Elizabeth Lesser

With the force of your slap, your punch, your put-down, I enter the wormhole and travel back to the Big Bang. I feel the blast of separation, the stunned particles of the embryonic universe rushing away from one another.

With the force of your slap, your punch, your put-down, I land in the dark mud, in the prebiotic soup where it all began—where the seeds of desire and conflict lay dormant and meaningless in the first cell. Pristine and glowing in its Oneness, yet somehow unfinished and clearly not thinking it through, the single cell made its fantastic leap into complexity, dividing into the chaos of otherness. And immediately, separation begat the longing for reconnection. Encased in a membrane, cut off from the mother ship, each self-reproducing cell slithered and crawled, flew and ran, propelled by a vague memory of fusion, of love, of Oneness.

With the force of your slap, your punch, your put-down, I feel into the first fish, first flight, first fuck. I am the original bird, the earliest monkey, primeval man, new woman—all relatives of the first atom, the first cell, all branded with an ache for union and a brain not big enough to map the way home. I am the half-baked heart of humanity, still evolving, ill equipped, attracted yet repelled by the other. I am yearning turning into taking; want becoming force; desire shape-shifting into greed. I am the first skipped beat of the heart, the first touch, the first kiss. I am gravity's pull toward love, and I am the weight of antimatter, tearing us apart. I know what happened first, and I know which force will prevail. I know how we got here; I know why the nations choose war; I know why you hit me. But I know what happens next.

With the force of your slap, your punch, your put-down, my eyes become clairvoyant, my ears supernatural, my mouth a time machine: I taste your father's violence, your mother's rage. I see your little spirit growing in the dark, feeding on crumbs, giving up, losing its instinct for love. I hear my little spirit whispering what it knows, saying it out loud, seeking approval, being shushed, christened bad, beginning to doubt. I see us forgetting—forgetting we ever knew how to sing. I am falling back, back before the forgetting. Past my submission, past your hubris, past your father, past my father and their fathers on back to the Big Bang, the first cell, the primal leave-taking, and the eternal return. I pass my mother, your mother, and their mothers, falling back and back and back, through centuries of horror and holy interventions, cycles of mistakes and corrections, generations of progress and loss: the brilliance of your sex squandered; the genius of my gender negated through the ages.

With the force of your slap, your punch, your put-down, I awaken. Delivered from the first fifteen billion years . . . just a blip after a bang! Just an awkward misstep as that first cell stumbled across the starting line. I'm taking evolution in my own hands now. It needs help. I know where we made the wrong turn—where the wires got crossed and instead of wooing the other into the bliss of union we went to war; we sought the One by hating the other, dominating the other, eliminating the other.

After your last slap, your punch, your put-down, I made my own fantastic leap: I walked out and never went back. I left you to do the holy work of your own transformation. I am no longer your tour guide, your evolutionary shepherd. Lying here alone on my bed, I run my hands over my breasts and vow to trust the milk and honey of my own heart. *I will make love with the other.*

I place my palm on my belly—where I am connected to God by a cord of blood and Eros. *I will follow* that *river*. My fingers explore the wet memory pool of my vagina, remembering and naming every tide that entered and each that left. Now I become the ocean; I become the wholeness: I am the being before the bang, the original soup, the earthy mess, the sweetest word, the warrior's sword, the angel's wing.

I am deciphering the DNA of destiny in a lab of grief and freedom. I am finding my voice. I have joined a choir of men and women who praise union without force, connection without submission. We crave the cliff; the time is now; the next fantastic leap!

Give It Back

Suheir Hammad

Give it
back how did you
get it give it
back you not using it
right no right to
it return it to
the earth to your
ancestors to the spirits
vanishing the physical

Enough allowance has been made for women
like you but genocide is
unacceptable you will
have to give it back
there are plenty of sweet gay
boys who could put it
to proper use and some women
would appreciate another
one just for fun

Give it up

You so awed with guns and
missiles put them down
there then and give back
what brings life

cherishes life
saves life

Your mama must not have told
you it was a gift
your time is up homegirl

Give it here yes
you are sorry no
you can't get it back
later

There are serious consequences remember?

Now get out my face with your
war whoring and don't come
calling when those bombs
and those guns are aimed at you

The Destruction Artist

Michael Cunningham

At first I just destroyed my own art. I'd do a painting, and I'd look at it and think, Right, another painting in the world, that's what we need. I felt this *shame* about it. Plus, okay, the paintings weren't that good. They were good enough. We're loaded with good-enough paintings and sculptures and installations and, you know, all that. Go to a dozen galleries. Nothing much is terrible. Nothing's great. It's all just good enough. You never feel like anybody died to make it. You never feel like it took a bite out of someone's soul and the wound will never heal.

So I started slashing up my canvases and breaking the stretchers and then burning the whole thing. I didn't want to just throw them away, I wanted them not to exist anymore. And it felt so good. It felt like I'd *done* something. It felt much better than not having made the paintings in the first place.

You can probably imagine what happened next. I started destroying other people's art. It was a natural progression. I was onto something, and it seemed too good to keep to myself. I could walk into a gallery and take care of a painting with a box cutter in, like, thirty seconds. I could stomp an installation into rubble like *that*. Sure, you get arrested, and charged with vandalism, and sued, and everything, but that's my art, that's part of it. And, you know, the artists don't like to admit it, but I make them more famous by wrecking their work. More or less the way a murderer makes his victims famous by killing them. But at the beginning, I only did inanimate objects. Cops and soldiers and psychopaths were so much better equipped for that other part.

And then, of course, an artist has to move on. The first few art attacks are exciting, they feel like something new, but by the tenth, it's over. So I started doing violence to myself. I started taking myself out of the world. Like we need another person, right? And, well, it's not like I'm that great. I'm not *bad,* I like myself well enough, but you know, I'm a shitty boyfriend and I'm pretty lazy and it's not like I'm contributing anything the world can't do without.

It was hard, the first time. I was scared. I knew I couldn't do an ear, an ear seemed like the least painful possibility, but it would've been derivative. It would've been misinterpreted. So finally, I worked up my courage, got a cordless buzz saw, took some Percocets with about a pint of vodka, went into one of the better galleries on a Saturday afternoon, took off my boots and socks, and cut off my left little toe right in the middle of the room. Most of you have probably never severed a body part. It's not as terrible as you might think. Your body does this *Whoa, wait a minute* thing, you get dizzy, everything goes sort of hot and white, there's this paralyzing whoosh of vertigo, but if you hold steady through that, your body kicks in to what I'll call mode two. *Right,* your body says, *left little toe's going, shut down the pain sensors, move into shock mode.* The real pain comes later, and it's not pleasant. But by then you've done it. You've done your art.

I'm in my last phase now, and it's the best work I've done. I had this final realization. If I haven't really done anything much for humanity, I can at least do my art in the service of others. So I don't perform the violence myself anymore. I invite other people to do it. It can't be just anybody. I screen *heavily.* No fetishists, no sickos, it's not about that. It has to be someone who's had violence done to them, and it's almost always women. Okay, it's always women. I've had male applicants, but I've always turned them down. It's not really something I can see happening between me and another man.

The women and I don't meet before, but we do agree on what will happen. My gallery handles that. The first woman—I don't tell their names—shot me, real carefully, in the shoulder, above my heart. Another woman buzzed off my right big toe, which was, as it happened, my last one. Another stabbed me in the back, right on the Magic Marker X, so she didn't get a lung or a kidney. And et cetera. It's up to them whether they want to talk after or just walk away. Some do, some don't. One woman held me and cried and asked me to forgive her. Which I did. One woman was pissed off, she demanded to know why I'd let her do a thing like that, but it felt like she was mad at herself and me both, as if we'd had sex when we knew we shouldn't, and were both to blame. I was down with that, too.

I'm pretty much done with the small stuff now, there's not really much more to give, so it's on to the next and, as they say, final step. I'm ready. I feel great. I feel clean and, I know this'll sound funny, *whole*. There's something saintly about it, like I'm sacrificing my body for something greater than me. I know that's a little bit blasphemous. Sorry, I'm not really a religious person. And, as you might suspect, there's not a big client base for the serious stuff. But it exists. Women are furious. Some are. You can't imagine what's been done to them.

If you're interested, ask around. You can probably find somebody who knows somebody who knows somebody. I'm still available. I'm here. I'm ready. I'm here for now.

Hands in Protest

Erin Cressida Wilson

An armless female soldier stands center stage. Her name is Michaela.

MICHAELA
"You fucking dyke." This is how the attack ended as I ran for the elevator and hit the down button, finally getting away from him. His attendant did nothing to help me, just stood watching as he pushed me up against the wall. I assume I was being called a dyke because I did not want to be raped by him. It was in the early evening, he had been out drinking with his full-time live-in assistant, who was there to watch over his abuses and wipe his ass. You see, he was in a wheelchair. And this, in itself, had put me off guard.

It had been a motorcycle accident five years prior. He had been poised for stardom. They say he had looked like Robert Redford.

But on this night, it was in a deserted hallway that he came off the elevator and lunged at me from out of his chair like a crazy screwed-up Spider-Man on LSD. I thought I noticed him hopping on one leg, but I didn't have time to put it together in my mind as he pressed me up against the wall.

I slipped away. With almost no struggle. And had no idea why until I looked back and noticed he was missing half his limbs.

So, how do you rape someone without your right arm and leg?

It's a funny story that I tell over drinks. Everybody laughs.

We even laugh at the "fucking dyke" part. I told this story over cocktails and torture in Iraq. With dust in my nose and liquor down my throat, I acted macho with the boys, showing off. They think it's hot when I say "dyke."

Ironic that I should lose my digits, too. And now I simply wonder how to mend the seam of an armpit, or how to stitch and embroider new limbs onto military ribbons and Purple Hearts. But mainly, I find myself worried. Wondering how to carry a baby without hands.

Do you pick her up by the scruff of the neck with your teeth? Then lick her diapers on? Do you feed her like a baby bird and learn to drink tea with your toes? Do you swallow bonbons sent by the media frenzy, and let male nurses drop them in your mouth while getting invitations to participate in the Special Olympics?

When an Iraqi holds up her hand, it means "hello," a greeting. My partner took it to say "stop," a threat. And shot her dead. Her whole family. Five bullets into them. And one of them was mine.

A trigger pulled by my fingers. From the hand that was blown off three days later. A land mine. And President Bush calls me a hero.

Sometimes I feel like my body parts are up for grabs. 'Cause if my arms hadn't come off but my tongue had been sliced out, what would I have done? I guess I would have turned my story into a song and sung it with my pussy on President Bush's front lawn. And then I'd have held a die-in on the final verse. If my feet had been burned, I'd have walked on my hands and blown smoke signals in the shape of peace signs. If my womb had been cut out, I'd have shocked him with my agitprop ways and made love to him with my eyes. If my eyes had been gouged out, I'd have put stars in my sockets and become the universe. And my ears? If they had been taken as trophies? If he had taken them instead of my arms? I'd start a silent protest. I'd hold your hand, and his hand, and her hand, and their hands, with my hands. I'd hold my hand up for you, a hello, a greeting. Not a threat. And I would not let go. Because they cannot, and will not, and are not ever allowed to break the bond between hands in protest.

Prayer

The Bra

Sharon Olds

It happened, with me, on the left side, first,
I'd look down, and the soft skin of the
nipple had become like a blister, as if it had been
lifted by slow puffs of breath
from underneath. It took weeks, months,
a year. And those white harnesses,
like contagion masks for conjoined twins
—if you saw a strap showing, on someone
you knew well enough, you could whisper, in her ear,
It's Snowing Up North. There were bowers to walk through
home from school, trellis arches
like aboveground tunnels, froths of leaves—
that Spring, no one was in them except,
sometimes, a glimpse of police. They found
her body in the summer, the girl in our class
missing since winter, in the paper they printed
the word in French, *brassière,* I felt a little
glad she had still been wearing it,
as if a covering, of any
kind, could be a hopeless dignity.
But now they are saying that her bra was buried
in the basement of his house—when she was pulled down into
the ground, she was naked. For a moment I am almost half
glad they tore him apart with Acteon
electric savaging. In the photo,
the shoulder straps seem to be making
wavering O's, and the sorrow's cups

are O's, and the bands around to the hook
and eye in the back make a broken O.
It looks like something taken down
to the bones—God's apron—God eviscerated—
its plain, cotton ribbons rubbed
with earth. When he said, In as much as ye have
done it unto one of the least
of these my brethren, ye have done it unto
me, he meant girls—or if he had known better
he would have meant girls.

Banana Beer Bath

Lynn Nottage

INSPIRED BY A TRUE STORY I HEARD IN UGANDA.

An attractive woman stands in a pool of light.

THE BEAUTY

And when asked . . . this is how the story will be told:

There were three beautiful women in the house near the top of the hill. The Elem sisters. The beauties. This was known as far down the road as a market woman could walk in one day. It was a fact, cherished by our village like the tasty banana beer made by my father. We, my sisters and I, lived in that house near the top of the hill, unaware of local envy or the mild scorn our beauty provoked. We simply looked like our mother . . . this is how we responded to compliments. Beauty didn't help us milk cows, dig roots, or make the sunset any later, so beauty was not something we needed. It was a treat that we allowed ourselves on market days. And yes, on our occasional walks to town that invited shopkeepers to rush to their doorways and blow warm-air greetings in our direction.

My father wasn't one to boast, but he knew we'd fetch a mighty fine dowry.

But here I'll jump ahead past the part of the story that doesn't really bear repeating, as we all remember the day when the rebels became more than market talk, and curious whispers gave way to civil war. When the wave of violence became too large to outswim, and swallowed our countryside. It is this part of the story that is repeated most often as a warning to children and unmarried women.

"They will beat you, rape you, and when they tire, they will kill you!"

"You'll be lucky if they make you a concubine or slave!"

Time and time again, the cruelties recounted. No, I won't repeat this part again.

Instead, here's what I remember, the snapping of twigs that announced their arrival just after sundown. We joked that it was the mischievous chimpanzee that liked to sip on my father's banana beer, but the insistence of the steps made my father believe otherwise. Shhhh. He blew out the candle. Shhhh. There were many of them on the wind, maybe twelve, fifteen in all, and they seemed to be moving with purpose. Shhhh. My mother quietly scooped up our warm dinners and dumped them into the latrine in the back. She rushed about our home looking for things to hide, whatever she could gather in a matter of minutes, anything and everything, working to erase our presence. Shhhh. Up the hill they marched.

"How do they know we are here?" asked Mother. Our house couldn't be seen from the road.

"They know," said Father. A curious look crossed between them. Mother fetched her celebration lipstick, smearing bright red color on her lips.

"Why are you putting on makeup, Mama?" I asked.

"We are expecting company," she said, and then rubbed shea butter on her face and body, giving her skin a robust glow.

We could hear rebels singing, a playful marching song, I think.

"They will beat you, rape you, and when they tire, they will kill you."

My father grabbed our arms, too tightly, and dragged us to the backyard where he kept the deep troughs of fermenting banana beer.

"Get in!" he whispered. "Get in!"

"No, it's too cold!" said my eldest sister.

"Get in, now!"

He thrust us into the trough, pushing our heads down into the cold ferment, and watched us sink into the sludge.

Then he covered the troughs with huge banana leaves and retreated into the house to wait. Wait. And wait. The singing was closer; we now could make out the lyrics of the playful marching song. We held hands, which we hadn't done in years.

"*They will beat you, rape you, and when they tire, they will kill you.*"

There we floated in banana beer, getting drunk on vapors.

We listened to the rebels move about our home, shouting for food! Money! Women!

"Where are they?" demanded a boyish voice.

"Who?" My father's panic drained him of authority.

"The three sisters, the beauties! We want them!" Our virginity was theirs, of course, and theirs to enjoy and ruin. The reward of war. They expected no less.

"There are no sisters left on this hill, just me," said my mother. "I am the beauty!"

And she offered her beauty to them. Laughter could be heard as they . . . raped her. She screamed, my father sobbed. We held hands tighter, sucking down beer to escape. Hours. The noisy forest rose up, and we knew our parents were gone.

We didn't dare move.

Imagine, for a moment, being betrayed by your own village elders. When I asked them sometime later, they argued that they were only protecting their own wives and daughters. We, the beauties, were their only offering, all they had to give of any value. Us.

Eternity. There, hidden away, numb, shivering, we floated in banana beer until morning light crested our hill and a day passed and another morning came in the same way. And then we heard them, footsteps approaching the trough, and we prepared to surrender our innocence. This was a moment we had known might come. We each gulped a huge mouthful of beer, preparing. Hours of our tears blended with the beer, giving it a familiar saltiness. Our hearts beat mad beats, angry, sad beats, bitter beats. The footsteps were above us, a lone figure cast a shadow across the banana leaves. We held our breath as a hand slowly lifted away our protective covering.

And then we saw the face of our discoverer. An ancient white bearded chimpanzee peered down at us, looking as surprised as we were. We could see the shock in her eyes. She hadn't expected to find us, the three beauties, soaking in beer. Her huge black furry hand reached toward us and then plunged into the liquid, scooping up a mouthful of banana beer. And then another, and then another. We watched as she grew pleasantly tipsy.

Then the chimpanzee gave us the most compassionate of looks, as if to say, "I understand." She carefully replaced the banana leaves overhead, and we listened to her disappear into the forest, and then . . . and then we found laughter in our throats, relief. And as if by invitation, we pulled ourselves from the trough of beer and staggered into the forest, drunk, wet, but very much alive.

True

Carol Michèle Kaplan

SPEAKER
(*in a rush of words*)
I saw a man in the park, his face bloated with anger, red, his arm
raised, the end of it a fist aimed at the child at his knees wanting
attention a hot dog I want something to eat I want I want but he
had nothing to give, no money no patience no anything else and
fury surged up in him as if from hell itself and the fist braced to
explode like a bullet and the little girl cringed and screamed,
"Please no don't!"
(*beat*)
And he didn't. He stopped. His arm frozen as if arrested by an
idea.
(*beat*)
And he looked at the little girl as if seeing her for what she was—
small, frightened, innocent—and he picked her up and tossed
her into the air and the little girl's laughter sounded like bicycle
bells and sparrows twittering in flight.

I saw this news report about Darfur that showed Janjaweed
militiamen riding their horses into the burning African village,
firing their automatic rifles at the scattering villagers—bare
backs, sandaled feet, ragged clothes whipping against bone-thin
limbs as they fled—and in one militiaman's path, an African
woman, a Zaghawan, eyes wide with shock, one hand stretched
out as if to fend off a blow, and at her breast, the nose of her
nine-month-old baby. And the soldier leveled the rifle and stared

down the barrel and the woman's whispered cry went out, "Please! No, don't!"

(*beat*)

And he didn't. He stopped. His finger poised as if caught by a thought.

(*beat*)

And he looked at the woman and saw her for what she was—a mother, desperate, alone—and he noticed that the other Janjaweed had passed and he spurred his horse on and galloped around her and the woman's sobs of relief rose up like the beating of drums strong enough to bring down the rains.

I read this article in a magazine where a Muslim girl, a Bosnian, just fifteen, was dragged from her bed and taken to a camp and surrounded by men who threatened to rape her and break her, who hit her and beat her, and she beseeched them, "Please no! Don't." And a teenage boy passing by heard her cries and he stopped. He came over to look and said, "I know you. We used to go to school together in Prijedor." He saw her for who she was.

And he turned to the men and said leave her alone she's just a girl from my school who won a prize for her essay and I've seen the sun shine on her teeth when she laughs with her friends, and the men hung their heads and backed away and the young girl's tears flowed like a prayer from her lips for the boy had appeared like an angel and intervened.

I knew a girl who went to school with me who always changed in the toilet stalls when we got ready for PE and one day she was late and couldn't wait and when she took off her shirt I saw welts on her back.

Red welts. The kind you can only get from a whip.

And she saw me see them and the look on my face and I stopped what I was doing and opened my mouth to tell her that I cared, that it was wrong, that we would confront her mother and shake the switch from her hand and fling it to the floor and stamp it into a thousand broken pieces and she'd never again have to fear going home.

(*beat*)

I wish this is the way things had happened.

Everything I have said, but they did not. No.

The father hit, the soldier fired, I did not speak I turned away I pretended I had not seen.

They did not happen as I have said, but they might have. Because of the boy from Prijedor.

He stopped.

He was the only one.

Club

Nicole Burdette

A Young Waif speaks:

Everybody loves stories about the eighties. Especially New York in the eighties. Here's one:

I was supposed to be in a fashion show at the Limelight. I had done them there before and gone in the back entrance but this time it was closed. I was nineteen years old and living at the Chelsea Hotel then and for some reason I was wearing a white fur coat—I still don't remember where I got it or where it went. In addition to the fact that I am allergic to fur. But regardless, I was wearing this coat with tennis shoes, white tennis shoes— I remember because at the end of this story I am sitting on the curb with my feet in the gutter on Sixth Avenue staring at my shoes. I was rushing, as I always was in the eighties, in New York. I went up to the main entrance and told the bouncer that I was in the show. He said the club wasn't open yet. I said "I know but I'm in the show and have to get in there," and then he hit me. (*Incredibly long, long beat*) (*Girl looks down, no expression*)

I'm sorry that I can't describe to you what it felt like. I can only say that I wanted to go back home in that moment and in that same moment I knew there was no home to go to—the hit didn't mean anything—was just a brutality—the bigger problem was where to go.

I made my way to the curb. I was in a daze and collapsed there in a pool of tears. There were so many homeless people that it was not unusual to see someone crying or lying in the gutter. I wish I could explain to you what it was like to sit in the gutter but all I could see were my tennis shoes—ghetto-white and brand-new. I remember this because I spent the first part of my life looking down at my feet. I could have been anywhere.

I didn't know where I was, I didn't know I was talking to myself—"I want to go home, I—I want to go home, I want to go home . . ." I was saying this all the while knowing I could never go back home. "I want to go to Minnesota . . ." (*Beat*) I knew there was nowhere to go—but I couldn't stop saying it and I couldn't stop thinking it. I couldn't move. (*Beat*) I was never a good girl in the sense that I could ever articulate what anything in my life had felt like. A hit was a hit. It didn't feel like anything. I was terrified to be awake in my life—I thought I would die. It was easier to look at the ground.

So the city, the gutter—everything turned white . . . landscapes of snow that seemed a long time ago. Meadows and flatlands and farms, cornfields high and bean fields . . . blankets of snow that went on for miles—a landscape so barren it looked like outer space. Following the lights along the highway, I saw the gas station five miles from my house.

By now I was far, far away from a gutter on Sixth Avenue. I was rolled up in a ball when I felt two hands on my shoulders. I heard, "Are you all right?" "What's happened to you?" "Honey, stop crying and tell me."

He had a kind voice I remember that. I didn't look up but I told him what happened. I let him pick me up out of the gutter and stand me on my feet. My knees gave out straightaway; he stood me up again and then he walked up to the club to have words with the bouncer—righteous and direct. Not violent.

Sixth Avenue was very busy now, wall-to-wall people, like it used to be in the eighties, but this man held me in his arms for a very, very long time—telling me it was going to be all right. I kept telling him I wanted to go home and he asked where that

was and I said I didn't know and that it was nowhere—that I
was hungry and tired and poor and that I was scared and that
I had been that way for a while, that I was so light that I could
float away or fall to the ground—what I couldn't tell him was
that I didn't see a way out of any of it—that I had just traded in
the barren landscape of my past for a more crowded, gray place
and that I could not find comfort anywhere in this world. I could
not stand up alone—my knees just kept buckling like a colt's. So
he waited and waited there with me until I could move. He
hailed me a taxi; he gave the driver some money and told him to
take me home. He told him to take good care of me.

About ten years later I was at a party. A woman I know
grabbed my arm and with great enthusiasm, smiling, said, "I
want you to meet my husband!" This man turned around. It was
him. He saw me and I saw him and we stared at each other. She
said, "Do you know each other?" And I said, "He helped me up
once." (*Beat*) "A long time ago."

Conversation Between Heaven and Earth

Kathy Engel

five years since I fell over the earth
forced myself to look at your made-up face in a wood box
it wasn't you
I delivered the eulogy
told how you rinsed the tomato sauce out of the spaghetti
for Naimah and Amandla
at Cummington when they were ten
you were trying to write as a mother does
Ajax in hand
Naimah has brought back your words to live forever
the story of women in prison

where are you at some ungodly hour when I need an ear for
    these words
can't go out there naked punctuation all crazy
you would say my clothes don't match
it is all a breaking of bars a planting of words a faith
    unimaginable
my arms around Naimah but I was pale she stood taller
than a young woman in your red dress taller than me
her pale aunt shrinking at that moment my voice caught
the way it did in childhood
at a grave site
poems or beauty don't bury
when Mbachi came from Zambia people thought
she was your daughter
this is relevant don't cut this line

our survival is relevant
our stories from Edgecombe Avenue   Zambia   Buffalo
and this Narrow Lane
are relevant
if I go to another meeting where men turn from naming
every rape I will

I know nothing new
wake in terror

did I tell you Naimah is strong and open
like rivers of Egypt we never swam
but dreamed of
we have always
carried bags   banners   babies on hips   backs   bellies
rinsed tomato sauce
have always cupped our hands like moons
to catch the wet crinkly utterance of life
crashing through dripping legs remember how you raced
to my baby shower late of course but with a basket of
    everything
I might need for the overflow
we have always melted the metal part of burning
into resistance

I can't possibly think of a new or original thing to say
but I just turned fifty and you left us at fifty
honestly I know less
question more
remember when we wrote a poem together about where we live
the black white beige and the food   children   Marvin Gaye

death penalties your black hands which are black
my beige hands living white
victorious in the holding
defying these cancers
except oh my if only you could see the girls now
you would sigh like the sun peeking through
the most glorious dawn because they are women and they
    know things
love to dance like we did speak Spanish
traverse continents they know something
poems roll like the sea
in your red dress
both girls wrote to you their aunt
we try to teach our children living something true but
    contradictions
eat our insides like Snickers bars
Naimah has three kids
sits at the computer with your words
her words
you wrote *everything sits on a minute*

minutes fall like Fallujah
at least you didn't have to see this
I recite the litany of brave women I practiced before birth
following your verse but the names scale down my body like
    skin
when I say *sister* we earned that
didn't name before earth tore open
to live
we who remain
suck poetry through veins

laugh volcanoes
laugh civil disobedience
pull onions from every sauce

drink
coffee in Gaza
grateful you didn't have to see hot sauce jazz blues raped
and they gave the storm a woman's name
grateful you can't hear the bombs again going down on ancient
  alphabets
like hard body parts into soft places

forced
your body left you
the cells testifying only against life finally
who legislates

this is all I can write at this hour of my life
love   poems   love   poems   resistance to cancer   resistance
  to war
resistance to stealing what we grow
resistance to leaving
resistance to hacking story like machetes

I know I need to talk about the place ghosts don't want to go
the naked place of responsibility
but all I can do is shake here in the middle of the night
in my drenching
dare the words
to come
drops of sweat and rain
orange light across our sky

I can't recall my grandmother saying the word *woman*
but that's what she gave me
my mother said *woman* told me never never let a person
with testicles lay a hand to you
come home to your mother you hear me that's the only rule

we have to do more than pray for our daughters
it is the middle of the night of my life
my sister is making fewer movies and more self-defense martial
   arts
she has babies
and a body

I'm holding my breath saying the names of our girls
the way you would
in my pajamas at 3 a.m. no more nightgowns
in the zone as you called it

a moment on heaven still on this earth still eating tomatoes
seeds we spit out as girls
fruit we loved as women
breathing horse whiskers we can be girls we can be women
we can be colors we never imagined the prison doors just
blew open your poems did that

IN MEMORY: SAFIYA HENDERSON HOLMES
DECEMBER 30, 1950—APRIL 8, 2001
(*with thanks to Alexis De Veaux*)

Part Owner

Dr. Michael Eric Dyson

Her body was never really hers to begin with. Sure, she may have had it for the twenty-seven years she's been on earth. But her body, like all black women's bodies, never really belonged to her. Or maybe it never belonged *just* to her.

When she said she was raped by three white men, it became very clear that her body isn't hers alone. It belongs to a history that hates black limbs and lusts for black flesh. It belongs to a politics that mutilates black souls and muffles black voices. It belongs to a nation that invaded black wombs for pleasure and profit.

Her body belongs to a nation that sold black bodies like cattle. It belongs to a court that said black folk had no rights that white folk were bound to respect. It belongs to a religion that said God saved African savages from their heathen homeland. It belongs to a region of citizens who went to war against their kin rather than give up the right to breed black bodies and keep them in bondage.

Her body belongs to every white man who wants it and who knows that a black woman can never be raped because she always "wants it." After all, she is a willing prisoner of her carnal urges. Why would three white men ever have to take what a black woman has always been willing to give?

Her body already belonged to them because their grandfathers had willed it to them, just as her grandfather had done the dirty work so they could be clean and comfortable. One of their friends reminded her just in case she forgot. "Tell your grandfather thanks for the cotton shirt."

She forgot that her body already belongs to them because the truth belongs to them. When a famous white man called her a 'ho on his radio show, he let her know that her body was his to play with and speak of as he liked. He could diminish her, even dismiss her, as he saw fit.

But her body also belongs to higher powers. It is on loan from the god who decided to give her life. At least that's what she's probably been told from the time she was a little girl. Back then theology made little sense except when there were stern reminders that "your body is a temple of the Holy Spirit."

If her family didn't tell her, the church did, even if she didn't sit in its pews. The black church shows up whenever black folks say that God told them to love you, or help you, or instruct you, or uplift you. It also shows up when some of them tell you that you're going to hell because you don't believe the way they believe. Or because you behave the way they *used* to behave before Jesus saved them from the lake of fire.

It shows up when sisters who mean no harm tell you to watch how you prance and switch. After all, if your body sways the wrong way, it might even sway holy men to forget that your body belongs to God. Next thing you know, they'll be borrowing his temple for a night and telling you that joy isn't the only thing that comes in the morning.

Her body also belongs to every music video that pictures her as a hoochie, or trick, or gold digger, or chicken head, or skeezer, or hoodrat, or slut. Her body belongs to the slow-motion frames that capture her breasts jiggling, her hips gyrating, her behind protruding, and her torso writhing in sensual conniptions. She belongs to every lyric that tags her "bitch" or " 'ho."

She also belongs to every voyeur who pounds his flesh in the dark to splash on her ebony eroticism. She belongs to every fantasy of furious sex conjured by the pulsating rhythms of pelvic thrusts. She belongs to every would-be stud who peels off his roll of one-dollar bills to stuff into her moving G-string.

She belongs to every woman who, in order to feed her children and put herself through school, has to dance for a living—either by twirling around a pole in a club or spiraling up corporate stairs to a glass ceiling. She belongs to every woman who has had to hear that if she hadn't been acting so sexy, she wouldn't have been raped.

But she belongs, even more, to black women. She belongs to that little black girl who was molested by her uncle and then intimidated into silence. She belongs to that black girl with budding breasts who was seduced by a man claiming to be her "play father." She belongs to that teenage black girl who was sexually abused by her mother's boyfriend and then thrown out of the house when her mother desperately needed to believe her lover more than her daughter.

She belongs to the black girl who committed suicide with her mother when they discovered they were both sleeping with the same married minister. She belongs to the black girl who was murdered by her mother's live-in companion because she might tell how he had taken her virginity when she was eleven. She belongs to the college student who was date-raped and hushed into shameful self-denial by repeating inside her brain all the reasons why she wasn't really raped. She belongs to those other young women who have to escort men in order to usher kids into adulthood. She belongs to those young ladies who are reprimanded by their elders with harsh judgment. "If you hadn't been acting like a loose woman in an immoral profession, you wouldn't have been abused."

If we never gain sight of her in all of this—never hear her voice or her story—she will only belong to myths and stories.

She will only be a symbol, a cautionary tale. But she is more than that. She is a flesh-and-blood woman who may have been washed away from her truest identity by a wave of hurtful headlines and hateful speech. When she gets over that, and over all of us, she will finally, perhaps even triumphantly, belong to herself.

Woman Work

Maya Angelou

I've got the children to tend
The clothes to mend
The floor to mop
The food to shop
Then the chicken to fry
The baby to dry
I got company to feed
The garden to weed
I've got the shirts to press
The tots to dress
The cane to be cut
I gotta clean up this hut
Then see about the sick
And the cotton to pick.

Shine on me, sunshine
Rain on me, rain
Fall softly, dewdrops
And cool my brow again.

Storm, blow me from here
With your fiercest wind
Let me float across the sky
Till I can rest again.

Fall gently, snowflakes
Cover me with white

Cold icy kisses and
Let me rest tonight

Sun, rain, curving sky
Mountain, oceans, leaf, and stone
Star shine, moon glow
You're all that I can call my own.

I've got to open the shop
Harvest the crop
Clean out the pool
Visit the jail
Get to the school
Teach all the classes
Pick up the mail
Raise food for the masses
I've got children to tend
The clothes to mend
I got to
I got to
I got to

Eye to Eye

Deena Metzger

In the dream, she can hear the moonlight fall, illuminating the black car that would have crawled silently as a shadow to her house perched at the end of a road where the last of the wild meets the encroachment of men. Or the vehicle, black as such vehicles are, and the windows dark to hide the occupants, is itself the instrument that slits apart the clouds to expose the light.

In the dream, she is awakened by silence rolling to her door and a man exiting the car soundlessly, as if he has learned from the animals how to walk, but he hasn't; he has learned only about boots and how to tread with them so nothing is signaled by his step. But the woman is awakened nevertheless because she knows the animal and this is no animal stalking. There is no kindness in the man and his approach, and so the woman waits for the door to open, the way ten or hundreds or thousands of women are waiting just then, somewhere, for such a door to open, a door she has a right to expect to remain closed, though it isn't locked because she hates splintered wood and shards of broken glass.

Everywhere women and girls, even young boys, are waiting for such an intrusion that can be described as bitter moonlight shining on a bayonet seeking the dark. A world, an entire globe, anguished by such a plague of waiting that until recently has never been afflicted so. The consequence of war, perhaps the very first world war, in interminable explosion.

Now, alert, she sits up and waits, the way a leopard unwinds itself from the tree branch that it embraces in its sleep, watchful for the first tremulous movement of air at the outskirts, and the first revelation of what is coming to the creature that can see in the dark.

She knows she will see before he will see, and this is not what he expects. She also knows he is blind, and he doesn't know he is blind. And so, having no weapons, and not wanting weapons, she will let him choose how he will have her, dead or alive. This choice will determine everything. And this, also, he doesn't understand.

In the dream, she speaks after he enters and makes his demands but also as if he has not forced his way, postured or blustered or puffed up like an adder. In the dream, she puts out her arms and raises her knees so the white nightdress falls between them like snow. In the dream, she does not allow him to kill her. In the dream, she draws him into her body with a tide he cannot resist.

In the dream, she takes him into her body—the young boy who has never been stroked, or who is tormented until he converts pain to pleasure, or who has not awakened from the nightmare in which, in order to live, he is forced to kill his sister and, in order to eat, to be a soldier for life.

In the dream, she takes him into her body—the mother who has watched this agony all her life. In the dream, she makes a demand that he cannot deny her. In the dream, he must look at her. In the dream, his eyes are open and locked into hers. In the dream, she does not blink, she does not falter. She does not lower her gaze.

In the dream, she cannot resist any more than the dry earth can refuse water, or the dark can refuse light, or the grave can resist the body that falls. In the dream, she decides to love him and to look him in the eyes. In the dream, he cannot look away.

In the dream, the rain falls on the bed, and embers of starlight burn onto the floor while the trees that were axed resurrect themselves from the stumps that remained, and the great cats roar again from their forest perch, and everything massacred rises up into life again.

Or it does not.

In the dream of a woman who had been raped twice—at knifepoint and at gunpoint—she takes the killer into her body and makes him look her in the eye. In the dream, she says, "You will have to claw your way to forgiveness." It is not the man's dream, and so we do not know if he understands. And then we do not know if the woman continues dreaming, or awakens, is awake, or if she dies.

Hail to the Vagina

Robert Thurman

The famous Indian Buddhist Esoteric Scripture, *The Glorious Esoteric Community Royal Tantra* (*Shri Guhyasamaja Tantraraja*), is presented as a revelation granted by the Primordial Buddha Vajradhara, who gives the teaching while said to be residing in "the Vaginas of the Diamond (Vajra) Female Buddhas" (*vajrayoshid-bhageshu vijahara*)."

This extraordinary setting essentially reveals the most profound nature of the infinity of reality, as perceived by enlightened beings, as the most sensitive, delicate, adamantine matrix of life and bliss. This most advanced esoteric text of the Buddhist inner science, then, describes the deepest absolute reality discovered by all fully enlightened beings, not as atoms or subatomic particles whirling dizzily about, not as a dark space of nothingness, not as inconceivable strings vibrating away in the eleventh dimension, but as "voidness the womb of compassion" (*shunyata-karuna-garbham*), "bliss-void-indivisible" (*sukhashunya-advaya*), i.e., as a delicate but ecstatically invincible envelope perfectly capable of holding all life in freedom from suffering, while nurturing it for blissful evolutionary fulfillment. It is utterly beyond all violence. A root Tantric vow is to never perceive any woman as unenlightened.

In Buddhist Tantric symbolism, the Victorious Vagina is represented as a (usually) red equilateral triangle with apex downward. It is called the Dharmodaya—Source of Truth, or Reality-Source. In Buddhist insight, there are two kinds of truth, absolute, ultimate, or actual truth or reality, and relative, conventional, or illusory truths or realities.

As the source of relative realities, the Dharmodaya Vagina gives birth to the world and all its beings and things, since things' freedom from fixated essence allows them to be created, develop, and flourish. This inexhaustible fount of creativity, when misunderstood, can be feared and hated as the source of suffering, since an alienated consciousness trapped in a fixated separated identity perceives the vast diversity of things as an overwhelming, uncontrollable opponent that cannot be either consumed or destroyed. But the real source of suffering is the misunderstanding, the ignorance, the misknowledge, not the Dharmodaya Vagina. When you have achieved transcendent wisdom, you emerge from the Vagina triangle, coming forward into the world and enjoying the magnificent diversity as the endless play of blissful energy. Only then do you truly *vive la différence*!

As the source of truth on the absolute level, we enter into the Dharmodaya Vagina triangle, go through it into the most profound transcendent reality of bliss-freedom indivisible. In this context, the triangle's corners represent the "three doors of liberation," three ways to approach the absolute freedom that is the ultimate reality of all things. These three are voidness, signlessness, and wishlessness, the visceral understanding of which leads to the enlightened realizations of freedom, peacefulness, and blissful satisfaction, respectively.

When you realize you are devoid of absolute, fixated, alienated essence, you discover the blissful freedom of infinite interconnection with all beings and things, a freedom that allows you to play harmoniously with all other relational things.

When you realize that each thing, just as it inconceivably is, is whole within itself as flowing nexus of interconnection with everything else, you are released from the compulsive drive to push it into processes of signification and causation, and you discover the unexcelled peacefulness of the reconciliation of all dichotomies and the adamantine tolerance of all cognitive dissonances that is enlightenment.

And when you realize that all beings and things are ultimately and primordially essentially fulfilled in their freedom and peacefulness, you discover the superbliss energy that is the actual reality of all things, and you effortlessly enjoy the wisdom of innermost, supreme, realistic satisfaction that transcends all suffering of both yourself and all others.

Within the sphere of the Victorious Dharmodaya Vagina, you live and die and live again endlessly without deviation from the Parinirvana play. As the great Kanhapa said, "I wander through the town adorned with my necklace of Parinirvana pearls!" This is utterly nondual and expresses the adept's experience that all of reality is a reliable matrix for the blissful communion of orgasmic bliss and peaceful freedom.

The two levels of truth or reality are only "levels," that is, different, on the relative, illusory level of conventional expressions. Ultimately, in their inexpressible actuality, they are indivisible, nondual. Thus relative superbliss and ultimate void freedom are indivisible in fact. The passionate red triangle represents this nonduality in that it can be entered into and emerged from simultaneously. This can also be symbolized by adding a second triangle, sometimes white, sometimes red, with apex upward. The nonduality then is represented as two intersecting triangles, which is familiar in India as Shiva and Shakti (God and Goddess, Peace and Power) in union, or as the domain of Chakrasamvara and Vajrayogini (Superbliss Machine and Diamond Unifier) in union, and in the West as the Seal of Solomon, or the Star of David.

However exactly we interpret the symbolism, however we rhapsodize about the Victorious Vagina, we cannot only adore its earthiness, we must celebrate its holiness, redolent with awesomeness and sacredness. Nothing profane or prosaic about it. Source of all happiness, violence can never reach it.

The Buddhist tradition is not mainly religion, however, does not mainly require belief, especially not belief in some fantasy world to be fabricated by suspending reason and straining the imagination. It is more science, encouraging reason, knowledge, and wisdom, considering that the more realistic you can be, the more genuinely happy and the more effectively benevolent you can be. So to truly enjoy the Victorious Dharmodaya Vagina, you need to know it deeply, to appreciate its magnificence and its profundity.

Hail to the Dharmodaya, Source of Truth and Mother of Bliss!

Rescue

Mark Matousek

I grew up in estrogen overload, in a house filled with difficult women, the only son of a harridan who'd sent her husband—my father—packing for love of another married man.

We were poor—not ghetto poor, but borderline white-trash Jewish poor: my mom, my three troubled sisters, and me, in our three small underfurnished rooms. For a long time—truthfully, my whole life—I'd convinced myself that this single fact of my boyhood, this isolation with too many women (picture a lost sperm circling an ovum), was the most formative piece of my story—hands down—the twist that made me *me* and formed my sperm-headed view of the world.

Then one day I realized that this was a lie—or should I say an incomplete truth.

I was in my shrink's earth-toned womb of an office. Martha was asking about my mother, who looms like Medusa over my insides, turning traitorous thoughts to stone. She knew about Ida already, of course, but not till that day had the question of rape been on the table. Ida was raped many times in her life—as a big-breasted girl running fast with Italians, as a teenage bride bartered to a sadist (to save what was left of her reputation), as a woman whose integrity, such as it was, pivoted in her own mind around being first and foremost an excellent fuck. These were the painful details I was sharing with Martha when she scrunched up her face all of a sudden and stopped me.

"You mother was raped?" she asked.

"All of the women in my family were raped," I told her.

Martha seemed shocked. I was shocked myself, not because

the information was new but because I'd never said it out loud, which meant it had only half existed.

Now that it did—now that I'd said it—a truth (so obvious that I'd missed it) blasted a hole through my story line, the version of things I'd believed to be true. It wasn't being trapped in a house filled with women that had made me the very strange person I was, but growing up in a houseful of raped women.

The nightmarish reel of flashbacks began, looking into Martha's eyes, pictures of naked female flesh, the pornographized landscape of childhood. But these pictures revealed themselves differently now, not as women whorishly wasting themselves (as others described it to me when I was a boy), not spreading themselves uncontrollably, prompting despair and abandonment; but as their bodies probably were, accosted, betrayed, and chewed up—discarded—largely against their will.

The images came back to me in a rush: my mother locked in the bathroom, weeping, hitting her head against the tub, whispering "I want to die" as I beat on the door and screamed till it opened—then her staring at me with dead eyes, a trickle of blood sliding down her neck from hitting her head against the enamel;

My beloved eldest sister, Marcia, escaping the husband who beat and degraded her, bound and gagged her, then dumped her for another woman and prompted her suicide at twenty-nine;

My other older sister, Joyce, being chased outside my bedroom door in the middle of the night, a strange man's voice coaxing, "I'm not gonna rape you," then disappearing at fifteen to a home for unwed mothers;

My baby sister, Belle, in hysterics at ten, crying to me that the neighbor whose child she babysat had been touching her in the bad place, wrong, and me confronting him (age thirteen) with a barbecue skewer on his patio.

These memories were just the beginning. There were more, there were echoes, the rapes continued—by men and soon enough by themselves, as my mother and sisters sold themselves short, raped their own choices, potential, respect; forced themselves into too-small, tawdry lives with men who used them as pleasure mules. The pictures came back, and as I described them—revealing so much more of the truth—a disturbingly different, more accurate picture began to emerge in myself *of* myself.

It wasn't estrogen overload that had turned me into a rescue artist; it was rape overload, abuse overload, an excess of feminine self-mutilation—an absence of innocent love toward a woman. Nowhere in retrospect was there a memory of woman adored, exalted, or blessed; nowhere an image of feminine eros protected, beloved, refined, rendered precious; and nowhere an entry for me to love in the way a boy (or man) needed to love in order to free himself of guilt: the guilt of not saving what he cannot save. The shame of needing to run away because he can't face the unsavable women. The disgrace of being forced to choose between himself, his life, and the women whose sacrifice freezes his heart, the heart he needs to survive—with despair.

Because these women were all I had. I loved them (in spite of everything) beyond words. For a long time this love was too much to face in light of the safety I could not give them. This was the actual bone-true story, I realized after that day in Martha's office, the kernel of mourning I'd buried in rage. I hadn't run away out of hatred. I'd run away from an excess of love.

This was shocking to me—this unmasking of grief. My armorial manhood began to unclench—forced me to share in their violation, to feel the assault on these women I cherished. Far easier to blame the victims than share their helplessness, I realized. But, telling this secret, I had no choice. There was nothing to hate now but violence itself, nothing to despise but men out of control, which plunged me into the heart of the matter. If men were rapists, then so was I (my childish black-and-white logic had told me long before I even had words for these things). As a fatherless kid starved for any male virtue to believe in—for faith in this sex I was born with, this stranger—I'd blocked the truth to save the faith that men could also be good and trusted, that I would never inflict such pain.

We do this, we men, very often, I think, mostly without knowing it. Every day in every country for every reason the mind can invent for why the violence is deserved. If Eve isn't guilty somehow, we wager—bringing the blood upon herself—Adam cannot rule the world. And so the blame-shifting lie continues till one day—if we're lucky and ready—we men drop the story, we start to grieve, and the cycle, the ignorance, comes undone.

I'd tell my story differently now if anybody wanted to hear it. I come from a family of raped women, but that no longer makes me a rapist. It makes me a man with a broken heart. I come from a family where cocks were weapons, but that does not make me a war machine. It makes me a man with a dangerous power (women have their own dark ways), equally fierce and beautiful. Now that I've grown into a man—now that I know I'm able to love—I can say what men do without hating myself or mistaking my power for violence. The tenderness of wolves, they call it— the exquisite absence of blood among killers. This is the tenderness men can give women. This is the story when shame finally ends.

To Stop the Violence Against Woman

Alice Walker

WOMAN

TO STOP THE VIOLENCE
AGAINST
WOMAN,
WOMAN
MUST STOP THE VIOLENCE
AGAINST
HERSELF.

WE CAN BEGIN TO DO THIS
NOW, NOW THAT WE SEE
A SKY
AND NOT A ROCK
A STICK
OR A FIST
ABOVE ALL
OUR HEADS.

WOMAN

TO STOP THE VIOLENCE
AGAINST WOMAN,
STOP THE VIOLENCE
THAT YOU
PERPETUATE
AGAINST
YOUR OWN

SISTER
WHO IS
A WOMAN, YOUR OWN
DAUGHTER
WHO IS
A WOMAN,
YOUR OWN
DAUGHTER-IN-LAW
WHO IS
A WOMAN.
YOUR OWN
MOTHER
WHO IS
A WOMAN.

WOMAN

TO STOP THE VIOLENCE
AGAINST WOMAN,
STOP THE VIOLENCE
THAT LIVES
IN OPPOSITION
TO YOUR LIFE,
DEEP IN YOUR
OWN TERRORIZED AND
UNCHERISHED
HEART.

WOMAN

REMEMBER WHO WE ARE:
NOT "GUYS"

BUT
THE MOTHER
OF ALL
LIVING.
WE CREATE OUT OF OUR OWN BLOOD
AND MILK
THE CREATURES
WHO OPPRESS
US;
WHETHER THEY ARE MEN
OR
OURSELVES.

WOMAN

AWAKE!
ARISE!
STAND UP!

WOMAN

TO STOP THE VIOLENCE
AGAINST
WOMAN,
GET UP
ON YOUR PERFECTLY
UNBOUND
FEET!
WE HAVE LOST THE EARTH
LIVING ON OUR KNEES.

Fur Is Back

Eve Ensler

I wanted to be funny. I wanted to be a funny, laughing, invited-to-the-party person. I wanted to be a little flirty, maybe, a little naughty, a little fab, mysterious, chic. I wanted to be fun—telling wild, crazy stories, jumping in the pool naked at midnight, wearing that sexy push-up bra. Driving the convertible fast down the highway in a rainstorm. I wanted to be delicious and adorable and not too available, not too talkative. I would have settled for a little dry, even, or sarcastic. Dry people get invited to the party. Dry nihilists, who are permanently unhappy, permanently in despair, bleak. They are there in their very expensive torn, shredded black clothing, surrounded by groups of beautiful people with fabulous torn, shredded haircuts that look like they just survived something awful—you know, that private jet ride where they ran out of merlot. But I am not dry. I am not adorable. I am not funny. I am angry. Fucking angry. I am raging.

I do not get invited to parties. Well, not anymore. I did at the beginning. I had a certain charm, a certain flair. People mistook it for funny until they discovered that I was the person who ruins the party. Interrupts the pleasure, brings in the rest of the world like a brutal Chicago winter wind. I am the person who, for some reason, has to see it, say it, and make everyone aware. I am the one who responds to the casual "what's up" with "Well, I just got back from Afghanistan, downtown Qandahār, where the Taliban is back. Where the Taliban actually never went away, but they are now blatantly back because the U.S. supported the wicked jihadis and put them in office. The jihadis who raped and pillaged and murdered and, instead of being brought to justice, were brought to power by the U.S., and now there is so much corruption and so much violence that the Taliban looks good.

I am that person who doesn't stop there, who has to go on because being at the party makes me even angrier. I somehow forgot until that moment that the rest of the world went on, went to the party, they were laughing, drinking, flirting, enjoying. They weren't undone or depressed by the whacked things going on. No the person asking me what's up didn't really expect an answer, didn't even particularly want an answer. Was just asking the question, a stupid party question 'cause that's what people do at parties. They don't listen, they don't give a shit, no, that's why they are at the party. That's why their whole life is a fucking party. Their whole life is directed toward getting invited to the party. Dressing for the party. Getting drunk or laid or into the party mood, and there I am ruining everything. What's up? What's fucking up? Don't you read the news? The Amish girls shot down in the school 'cause they were there, 'cause they were girls. Or the girls in the refugee camps in Darfur going to get grass for their donkeys or wood for the fire who get grabbed, who get raped and raped and can't find their way back. But let's protect the rapists, okay, let's defend them like the cleric in Australia said. They are being given too hard a time, a terrible sentence, when it's really the woman's fault, she brought it on herself, they brought it on themselves by not wearing a head scarf. They were open meat. If she had just stayed in her home, in her hijab, there wouldn't have been a problem. The cleric saying this—in 2006. If they had just stayed at home.

If I had just stayed at home, hadn't gone out, hadn't opened my mouth. I wasn't even invited to this party, a friend was invited and took me 'cause she couldn't find anyone else. It wasn't a direct invitation, a primary invitation from the source to me,

and I am ruining the party, embarrassing my friend. I shouldn't
have gone out of the house. There were too many bad things
happening. Maybe it was hearing the woman at the party with
the big stuffed thing around her neck say, "Isn't it fabulous—fur
is back." Fur is back. Isn't it fabulous? Mutilation is back. Murder is back. Mink is back. Mink always makes me think about
women. Not just that women wear minks, but that there is
something about how women are raised to serve. Raised for
slaughter. Something about being so beautiful, so soft and warm,
that people have to wear you, have to wrap you around their
neck or rape you from behind or shoot you in the head or man-
gle or beat or starve you.

Fur is back. Fur is back. Isn't it fabulous, fur is back? So, it
turns out, is rape. Rape is back. The Taliban is back. O.J. is
back. Fur is back. Back back back.

But when did any of this go away? It never went away. It just
gets ignored and buried and accepted by the people at parties, by
the people who cannot stop partying, who think that life is one
big party, which it is for them because they have everything, because they are wealthy and privileged and perfect and partying
partying. Stop it. Stop it. Please please stop. Women are dying.
Women have their labia ripped off in the Congo, their faces
melted off in Pakistan, they are bought as children in Atlanta.
Stop, please, doesn't it matter to you? Don't their lives matter? I
am screaming. I am on the floor, on the wall-to-wall plush carpet
near the buffet table with its goat cheese quesadillas and grilled
shrimp and chocolate martinis. I am on the floor screaming, Stop
it, stop it.

Stop. Can't you just stop? For one moment, stop your lives,
stop your quest for pleasure, stop your partying. A crowd is now
looking at me, a crowd of fabulous partygoers who won't look
directly at me 'cause they are scared they might catch what I

have, fabulous partygoers going on as I am being handcuffed, dragged, and removed from the party. I don't move, I can't move. I lie there on the street against the building and I open my eyes. I am looking up, straight up. I don't remember seeing stars before in the city. There are so many of them and they are particularly sparkly. I don't know if they are even real. They are so far away and they are right next to me. I am lying there and my eyes are open. I am not funny and my friend's silk shirt is torn, but I can see what is in front of me. I can see the stars.

Afterword: Reclaiming Our Mojo

Jane Fonda

> Every mother contains her daughter in herself and every
> daughter her mother and every mother extends backwards
> into her mother and forwards into her daughter
>
> —Carl Jung and Carl Kerenyi, *Essays on a Science of Mythology**

It would have been easy to miss altogether. Just a short sentence
tucked within the fifty or so pages of my mother's medical
records:

*"She spoke with considerable shame of being molested at age
eight."*

The moment I read it, I was filled with relief. Yes, sadness for
her. Of course. Sadness. I wanted to hold her and rock her and
tell her I understood and forgave her. But relief was there, too,
flooding me as I lay shivering in the bed.

I was two years into writing my memoirs, *My Life So Far,*
which I dedicated to my mother as a way to force myself to discover why she was the way she was. Part of that research meant
trying to obtain her records from the institute where she committed suicide in the late 1940s on her forty-second birthday. I
was twelve.

The evening the records arrived, I had to climb into the bed
and cover myself in blankets because I suddenly felt so cold.
Here were the documents that would enable me to travel back in
time into the reality that had been the last days of my mother's
life. What I had not anticipated was that there, tucked away

*Bollingen Series 22 (Princeton: Princeton University Press, 1963), p. 162.

amid the daily reports from doctors and nurses about her deteri-
orating state, was her own eleven-page double-spaced autobiography. Could it contain the clues to the puzzle that I needed?

Perhaps other family members had read these documents
before me and missed that one sentence. Or had read it and not
paid it much heed. Not understood what she meant when, in re-
counting her middle and high school years, she wrote, "Boys,
boys, boys." Not connected the dots upon reading that she'd
had six abortions and plastic surgery before I was born in 1937,
and that her psychiatric tests at the end were "replete with per-
ceptual distortions many of them emphasizing bodily defects and
deformities."

But I had been getting ready for this moment for years and
could at last understand and forgive her and, in doing so, forgive
myself.

All my adult life, I had wondered about my mother's childhood. The older I got and the more I understood about the long-
term effects of early trauma, the more I intuited that something
bad must have happened. Maybe that was why I had been
drawn to studying childhood sexual abuse over the previous five
years. Maybe that was why in 1995 I founded the Georgia Campaign for Adolescent Pregnancy Prevention and soon discovered
that childhood sexual abuse was the single biggest predictor of
teenage pregnancy. Sixty percent of teen mothers fifteen years
old and younger have been victims of sexual abuse.

By the time I read my mother's reports, I knew that sexual
abuse, be it a onetime trauma or a long-term violation, is not
only a physical trauma but that its memories carry a powerful
emotional and psychic charge and can lead to emotional and
psychosomatic illnesses and difficulties with intimacy. The ability
to connect deeply with others is broken, and it becomes difficult
to experience trust, feel competent, have agency. I knew that sex-

ual abuse robs a young person of a sense of autonomy. The boundaries of her personhood become porous, and she no longer feels the right to claim her psychic or bodily integrity. For this reason, it is not unusual for survivors to become promiscuous starting in adolescence. The message that abuse delivers to the fragile young one is "All that you have to offer is your sexuality, and you have no right to keep it off-limits." *Boys, boys, boys.*

Then there's the issue of guilt. It seems counterintuitive that a child would feel guilty about being abused by an adult whom they are incapable of fending off. But children, I learned, are developmentally unable to blame adults. They must believe that adults, on whom they depend for life and nurture, are trustworthy. Instead, guilt is internalized and carried in the body, often for a lifetime, often crossing generations—a dark, free-floating anxiety and depression. Frequently, this leads to hatred of one's body, excessive plastic surgery, and self-mutilation (more and more, I feel they are the same).

But the most profound thing I learned—years before I'd read my mother's history of abuse—was that these feelings of guilt and shame, the sense of never being good enough, and hatred of one's body cast a long shadow that can span generations, carried on a cellular level to daughters and even granddaughters.

Mother saw many doctors and psychiatrists for a seemingly endless list of ailments. As a child, I had begun to believe that she liked being in hospitals more than she did being home. But in those days, if the doctors had thought to connect her medical issues with early sexual abuse, which was unlikely, they certainly wouldn't have known what to do about it.

The psychiatrists she saw would have been Freudian. She'd have lain on a couch, staring at the ceiling, with the doctor sitting silently behind her. Just what she didn't need. As Dana

Crowley Jack has said, "the more traditional therapy reproduces a hierarchical relationship of authoritative (male) therapist and deferential (female) client which is not conducive to relationship."

Early on, Freud had discovered incest and sexual abuse as the root cause of what was then called "hysteria" among his first well-to-do female patients. When his theories about this were first published, he was ridiculed by his colleagues in the field, who said it was unthinkable, an impossibility. Doubting his conclusions and perhaps fearing they would prevent his rise within academia, he developed what became the classic Freudian theory: Children *want* to have sex with their parents, and when incest is reported by patients, it is to be seen as sexual fantasy.

From then until the 1970s, the psychiatric profession firmly believed that incidents of sexual abuse and incest were "one in a million." The frequency and effects of such trauma (and the ways to treat it) did not begin to surface until the arrival of a new wave of pioneering feminist psychologists such as Carol Gilligan, Jean Baker Miller, and Judith Lewis Herman. Only in the 1970s, when women began to eschew the old presuppositions (*one in a million!*) and listen to one another empathically, did the truth emerge: Childhood sexual abuse and incest were and are epidemic.

These women and their colleagues were also discovering that recovery required rebuilding bonds of trust and connection. Because so many survivors of childhood violence, sexual abuse, and incest have experienced trauma at the hands of a loved and trusted person, closeness to another can come to represent danger. Intimacy, for them, is too frightening, and so they cut off. We can cut off, deny, and be symptom-free, but the shadow is there, tamping down our potential juice—muting our mojo. The shadow becomes all the darker and more powerful when we deny it.

With the birth of relational psychology, the landscape of treatment for survivors of abuse has been transformed. Rather than the former neutral, impersonal form of psychotherapy, it is through the empowerment of a trusting, growth-fostering relationship that the damaged faculties allowing us to experience intimate connection can be brought back to life.

I often imagine how it might have been for my mother had she lived today and had the support of a community of women who could have heard her story, believed it, and been moved by it. The alchemy of their tears might have opened her heart to her own pain.

That's the crucial step.

I have a friend whom I love very much. He once told me about his childhood, describing without the slightest affect a litany of psychological and physical brutality. He seemed surprised when tears began rolling down my cheeks.

"But it was for my own good!" he declared, assuring me that the perpetrator was his "best friend." Try as I might, I was never able to help him move through the factual history and reconnect with his feelings as that young boy, so beaten and abandoned. Nor could any therapist he saw over time. Perhaps the wounds were too deep, the scar tissue too thick. Besides, to the world, he seemed to be getting along just fine—no visible symptoms. Only those who wanted a deep connection with him knew why he couldn't show up, why the empathy gene seemed to have been plucked from his heart. He could not experience empathy for others or for himself. As I've discovered, healing often has to start with self-empathy.

It is too late for my mother. But not for me. I feel blessed to

have been given the truth about her history because it has enabled me to understand her as well as the nature and cause of my
own shadow.

Isn't it our job in life to get out from under the shadow and
reclaim our mojo, realize our full potential as human beings?
Don't we—don't I—need to expose the shadow to the light? Isn't
this the greatest legacy we can leave our children?

I have already made big strides. I have written my memoirs,
my own historical narrative that reaches back to my ancestors
and forward to my children and grandchildren—the remembering part. I feel this is a gift to them. When I die, or maybe even
sooner than that, they can use my narrative, as I used my
mother's, to shed light on their own.

My task now is to go beyond the narrative and to enter it ex-
perientially, emotionally. Memory reconnected to feeling.

I know many people who have been able, with help, to move
beyond dissociation. I'm one of them, and I've learned it's an ongoing journey, not easy in a patriarchal culture that tells us it's
better to stuff it. Maturity, we're told, means staying always in
control.

But what's so great about control if your heart feels empty
and the walls between you and others feel impenetrable? Step
three in AA's twelve-step program is about giving up control to a
higher power. For me, right now, my higher power is my own
deep consciousness, my own Divine within that needs me to surrender to it the tightness and brittleness of control.

I'm in the last act of my life. What frightens me isn't the
thought of dying but getting to the edge of life with regrets. I discovered in preparing for my last act, at age sixty, that my biggest
regret would be to have never experienced real intimacy. To do
this, I saw, to finally overcome my fears, I would have to be will-

ing to go to that dark, shadowy place and experience it. To learn to acknowledge and handle the toxic parts of what I inherited from my mother but also embrace and embody the juicy, sensual, wild, and beautiful parts of her. I can't do this if all I have is a relationship to the facts.

Knowing and healing aren't the same. We can talk about the facts of trauma, recount the chronology, and still continue to be cut off from the experience, unable to go back to the dark place and feel. Healing takes feeling.

Healing also takes courage, because it's painful.

But if you've ever exercised for physical fitness, you know the difference between the pain of hard muscular or anaerobic work and the pain of injury. The former has a positive payoff: increased strength and fitness.

So it is with the pain of the internal work required for recovery. Yes, it's painful to purposefully try to access the emotions of trauma. But out of the pain can come a new, deeper, freer life if you are in a safe place, with loving guidance from a knowledgeable, skillful therapist or with a professionally guided group of women on the same journey.

For many, bodywork and holotropic breathwork, as developed by Dr. Stanislav Grof, and other transpersonal psychotherapies can dislodge the blockages that prevent us from reexperiencing and integrating early trauma.

It's important to create an intentional community of love, friends who are also committed to living as fully and wholly as possible. Eve Ensler and I are part of each other's community of love. It was with her that I first witnessed the power of what I call therapeutic listening. We were visiting a shelter for abused and abandoned girls in Jerusalem. Eve had asked permission to interview five or six of the girls, and I was worried that in the brief several hours we had with them, we would be opening Pandora's box and then we'd be gone. That's not at all what happened.

I saw what is meant by "active listening." Eve pulled the girls into the act of remembering and encouraged them to go beyond the unspeakable facts of their traumas to what their feelings were. Her listening always held palpable respect and empathy. She shed tears for them, and a shift occurred. I could feel it: Each girl saw she was believed and began to hear her own story with empathy. For the first time, the girls heard one another's stories, and this, too, seemed therapeutic. A community had been created.

Serendipitously, I recently made a film that touches on the subject of incest. At dinner one evening with one of the producers, I was talking about the frequency of sexual abuse and incest and how so many women I know—most, in fact—have experienced this trauma.

"Why is this?" he asked. "Don't tell me it's about power."

Don't tell me it's about power.

I saw that evening how dissociation can happen not only to victims of trauma but on a mass social level. This is how we avoid seeing violence against women as an inherent part of male dominance—the drive to impose power over those society views as "less than," or the drive to ensure submission of those whose power is feared.

A psychiatrist once said, "The general contractor for the social construction of masculinity and femininity is psychological trauma, but the architect is the system of dominance."*

---

*Bessel A. Van der Kolk, "The Body Keeps the Score" (Cambridge, Mass.: Harvard Medical School, 1994), p. 219.

In case you think that in the United States at the beginning of the twenty-first century women aren't viewed as less than, listen to how men put down other men by calling them "girls," "pussies." How men who exhibit wonderful qualities such as empathy, compassion, nurture, qualities associated with women, are often scorned. And that's without going into issues like lower pay for comparable work and far lower representation in the halls of corporate, media, and political power.

For survivors of violence, sexual abuse, and incest, part of what can lead them to self-repossession is to be drawn into the work of stopping the violence—like Eve Ensler has done. This can mean supporting shelters for victims of rape and domestic violence, creating crisis hotlines and rape crisis centers where there are none. We must ensure the presence of victim advocates in the court system, and the enforcement of penalties against perpetrators.

Those are some of the immediate forms that healing activism can take. But we need to hold in our hearts a bigger vision of a world in which both men and women are able to be full human beings, in control of their bodies and their hearts, respecting others' bodies and hearts. And the more we achieve that within ourselves, the more effective we'll be at moving society into a post-dominant era.

An Invitation: How to Get Involved

The writings in *A Memory, a Monologue, a Rant, and a Prayer* were first presented in June 2006 as part of a theater and film festival called "Until the Violence Stops: NYC," which invited all eight million New Yorkers to stand up and join V-Day, a movement dedicated to stopping violence against women, to make New York City the safest place on earth for women and girls.

The Issue: Violence Against Women

The goal of "Until the Violence Stops: NYC" was to bring the issue of violence against women and girls front and center. In order to understand the grave importance of this cause, one must know that violence is an issue that plagues all women in every part of the world. To better show the depth and epidemic scope of violence against women, V-Day has compiled a list of statistics and resources that demonstrate the impact of violence against women on the individual and the community.

International Facts: Violence Against Women Is a Global Issue

- At least one in three women has been beaten, coerced into sex, or otherwise assaulted in her lifetime.[1]

1. Amnesty International, launch report, "It's in Our Hands: Stop Violence Against Women," 2004.

- Two million girls are at risk for female genital mutilation each year.[2]
- Seventy-nine countries have no legislation against domestic violence.[3]
- Violence against women is most prevalent in Latin America, Africa, North America, Australia, and New Zealand.[4]
- Fewer than one in three female victims of violence report their victimization to the police.[5]
- Globally, fewer than half of the victims who reported their cases to the police were satisfied with the response.[6]
- About half of women surveyed believe it is acceptable for a husband to beat his wife under certain circumstances.[7]

National Facts: Violence Against Women Is a U.S. Issue

- Nearly one third of American women report being physically or sexually abused by a husband or boyfriend at some time.[8]
- Someone is raped in the United States every two minutes.[9]

2. A. Lewnes, "Changing a Harmful Social Convention: Female Genital Mutilation/Cutting," *Innocenti Digest* 12, October 2005.
3. Amnesty International report, "The State of the World's Human Rights," 2006.
4. Sushma Kapoor, "Domestic Violence Against Women and Girls." Preliminary Edition. UNICEF/*Innocenti Digest* 6, June 2000.
5. United Nations Crime and Justice Information Network overview (www.uncjin.org/CICP/cicp.html#overview).
6. Ibid.
7. World Health Organization, "Multi-Country Study on Women's Health and Domestic Violence Against Women," 2005, chapters 3 and 4.
8. L. Heise, M. Ellsberg, and M. Gottemoeller. *Ending Violence Against Women. Population Reports, Series L,* no. 11, December 1999.
9. U.S. Bureau of Justice Statistics, *National Crime Victimization Survey,* Criminal Victimization, 2005.

- One in four women will experience domestic violence in her lifetime.[10]
- Homicide is the leading cause of death for women on the job in the United States.[11]
- From 1976 to 2002, 81.1 percent of female-victim homicides in the United States were sex-related.[12]

New York City Facts: Violence Against Women Is a Local Issue

- In 2004, the New York City Domestic Violence Bilingual Hotline received 155,375 calls, a 36 percent increase over 2003.[13]
- Each year there are a reported 584 murders, 2,015 rapes, and 20,702 felonious assaults in New York City.[14]
- Every year fifty thousand people, mostly women and children, are forcibly brought to the United States. Many of them end up in New York City, working for little or no money as prostitutes, domestic workers, and sweatshop workers.[15]

10. Patricia Tjaden and Nancy Thoennes. National Institute of Justice research report, "Extent, Nature, and Consequences of Intimate Partner Violence," July 2000.
11. "Violence in the Workplace: Risk Factors and Prevention Strategies," National Institute for Occupational Safety and Health—DHHS (NIOSH) Publication no. 96–100, July 1996.
12. U.S. Department of Justice, Bureau of Justice Statistics, 2002.
13. Urban Resource Institute (www.uriny.org/dvHome.php).
14. New York Police Department, "CompStat Unit Report," vol. 10. no. 14, 2002.
15. Francis T. Miko and Grace (Jea-Hyun) Park, Congressional Research Service, report for Congress, "Trafficking in Women and Children: The U.S. and International Response," March 18, 2002.

Workplace Facts: Violence Against Women Is Expensive—
Physically, Emotionally, and Spiritually—for All of Us

- The Centers for Disease Control and Prevention have estimated that the annual cost of lost productivity due to domestic violence equals $727.8 million, with more than 7.9 million paid workdays lost each year.[16]
- The national health care costs of domestic violence are high, with direct medical and mental health care services for victims amounting to nearly $4.1 billion.[17]
- Ninety-four percent of corporate security directors surveyed rank domestic violence as a high security problem at their company.[18]

Prison Facts: Violence Against Women Breeds Violence

- Forty-eight percent to 88 percent of women inmates in the United States had experienced sexual or physical abuse before coming to prison (as many as 90 percent in New York and Ohio prisons) and suffer post-traumatic stress disorder.[19]
- An estimated 56 percent of the abused women in prison said that their abuse had included a rape, and another 13 percent reported an attempted rape.[20]

16. "Costs of Intimate Partner Violence Against Women in the United States, U.S. Department of Health and Human Services, Centers for Disease Control and Prevention, 2003."
17. Ibid.
18. Ibid.
19. Amnesty International USA, "Women in Prison: A Fact Sheet" (www.amnestyusa.org/women/womeninprison.html).
20. Trace L. Snell, Women in Prison, Survey of State Prison Inmates, 1991. Bureau of Statistics: March 1994, p. 6.

V-Day. A Movement to End Violence Against Women

Founded in 1998 on the principle that art inspires activism, V-Day is a global movement to end violence against women and girls that raises funds and awareness through benefit productions of Eve Ensler's award-winning play *The Vagina Monologues*. V-Day is a catalyst that promotes creative events to revitalize the spirit of existing anti-violence organizations and generates broader attention for the fight to stop violence against women and girls, including rape, battery, incest, female genital mutilation (FGM), and sexual slavery.

Through V-Day campaigns, local volunteers and college students produce annual performances of *The Vagina Monologues* to raise awareness and funds for anti-violence groups within their own communities. In 2006 more than 2,700 V-Day benefit events were produced by volunteer activists in the United States and around the world, educating millions of people about the reality of violence against women and girls.

Performance is just the beginning. To date, the V-Day movement has raised more than $40 million and educated millions about the issue and the efforts to end it. V-Day produces large-scale benefits and innovative gatherings, films, and campaigns to educate people and change their social attitudes, including the documentary *Until the Violence Stops*; community briefings on the missing and murdered women of Juárez, Mexico; the December 2003 V-Day delegation trip to Israel, Palestine, Egypt, and Jordan; the Afghan Women's Summit in Kabul; the March 2004 delegation to India; the European Organizer Workshop in Brussels in March 2005; the Stop Rape Contest; the Indian Country Project; and Love Your Tree.

V-Day has crafted international educational, media, and PSA campaigns, launched the Karama Program in the Middle East, re-opened shelters, and funded more than five thousand community-based anti-violence programs, as well as safe houses in Kenya, South Dakota, Egypt, and Iraq.

V-Day events have taken place in all 50 United States and in more than 112 countries from Egypt to Australia to Kenya to the Philippines.

Today V-Day is a model of empowerment philanthropy and public awareness, inviting women and men to use art and performance to raise funds and awareness in their own communities. The V in V-Day stands for "Victory," "Valentine," and "Vagina." To learn even more about V-Day, go to www.vday.org.

Until the Violence Stops: The Festival

Conceived by its founder, Eve Ensler, and produced by V-Day in June 2006, "Until the Violence Stops: NYC" brought the issue of violence against women and girls to the New York City streets, subways, and buses, putting women, their empowerment, and safety at center stage. This New York City–focused campaign utilized the key elements of performance and theater to raise consciousness and funds and expand the dialogue about violence against women and girls locally, nationally, and globally.

With marquee events, performances by celebrated actors, original works by noted authors, community involvement throughout the five boroughs, a citywide advertising campaign, and a run through Brooklyn's Prospect Park, "Until the Violence Stops: NYC" issued a call to action not just to all New Yorkers, but to the whole world: Demand a halt to violence against women and girls and become an active participant in ending it.

"Through V-Day, we have witnessed the power of art to transform and galvanize change," stated Ensler. "It's time to be bold, to amplify our efforts, and to take our movement to end violence against women to the next level. V-Day was born in New York City, and 'Until the Violence Stops: NYC' took our message directly to the people of New York. Together, we will make New York City the safest place on earth for women and girls."

Joined by artists and community organizations, V-Day worked to raise the awareness level in New York City, educate people about violence against women and girls, and encourage citizens to take action to end it. We are poised at a historic moment for women and girls worldwide, and the festival was an unprecedented opportunity to create change around the issue of violence against women and girls.

As with the V-Day model established with *The Vagina Monologues,* "Until the Violence Stops" was designed to be replicated. Following the success of the festival in New York City, activists in Kentucky and Ohio are producing "Until the Violence Stops" festivals in their communities in summer 2007, and festivals are being planned for 2008 in select cities including Paris, Los Angeles, and Providence, Rhode Island. All festivals will be produced locally, with local talent and highlighting local anti-violence groups, under the guidance and support of V-Day.

Action: You Can Help End Violence Against Women and Girls

Here are the simple concrete steps that can change the world—your world:

Produce a V-Day Event in Your Community

V-Day revolves around art and activism, using theater as a grassroots mechanism to raise awareness and funds. There are three ways to produce a V-Day event in your community:

1. Stage a Reading of A Memory, a Monologue, a Rant, and a Prayer

The essays in this anthology make for a powerful evening of theater and action. Below we have provided you with a brief outline of what it takes to have a successful benefit performance of this evocative piece. Contact V-Day for guidelines, direction, and rights by e-mailing memory@vday.org.

- *Sign up with V-Day.* To be an official organizer, you must apply to V-Day. Organizers must be approved by V-Day, and the script and an organizer materials kit will be made available upon your signing up.
- *Assemble a production team.* You will need a core group of dedicated volunteers to help you produce your event. Invite as many people as you can: women and men of all ages with different backgrounds, interests, and skills.
- *Secure a venue and reserve dates.* Don't underestimate the number of people who will want to come to your event. Try checking with your city's parks and recreation offices; they can tell you about venues that aren't common knowledge and might be more affordable for charitable events. Research publicity, support, and other resources. Are there props available that you can use? Is there an in-house stage manager? Sound technician? Lighting? Investigate your options to make sure you are getting the best resources at the best cost.
- *Secure a fiscal sponsor and pursue event sponsors.* Your event should have both a fiscal sponsor and an event sponsor (who may or may not be the same). A fiscal sponsor is a qualified nonprofit organization that provides the financial administration and oversight necessary for your event to receive tax-deductible donations. This will enable your event to have nonprofit status as well as permit donors to claim the tax

deductions to which they are entitled. The event sponsor is a person, organization, or business that supports the show financially or provides performance space, production assistance, or other in-kind support.

- *Select beneficiaries.* Beneficiaries should be qualified 501(c)(3) organizations in your community that are already working to stop violence against women and girls or are providing direct aid to victims. Such organizations include battered women's shelters, rape crisis centers, stop-rape education programs, and similar direct service programs for women and girls.

- *Secure a rehearsal space.* It will be important to secure a reliable and adequately sized space in which you and your team can work and create comfortably.

- *Hold auditions.* Publicize your auditions and be sure to welcome everyone who is interested, regardless of acting experience.

- *Organize fund-raisers.* Raise money for your production by holding fund-raisers, such as film festivals, concerts, silent auctions, dance parties, and bake sales.

- *Get the word out about your event.* Create and distribute posters, fliers, brochures, postcards, and so on. Be sure to follow V-Day's identity guidelines; contact press@vday.org for more information.

- *Create press releases and contact media outlets.* Use your event to raise awareness about violence against women by publicizing the event in local print, radio, television, and Internet outlets. Be sure to include local statistics and information from your beneficiaries about violence in your own community.

2. Stage a Festival: Bring "Until the Violence Stops" to Your Community

"Until the Violence Stops" is a two-week awareness and fund-raising festival. By gathering anti-violence artists, actors, business, and civic leaders in your community, you can make a difference. To learn how to produce the festival in your community, contact festival@vday.org. V-Day provides guidelines to producers, organizations, and local activists.

3. Stage a V-Day Benefit of The Vagina Monologues

Every year V-Day benefit productions of playwright/founder Eve Ensler's award-winning play *The Vagina Monologues* take place at thousands of locations around the world, raising money for local organizations in their communities that are working to end violence against women and girls. Local college students and local community activists and volunteers organize these events—people just like you. The event can be large or small; the impact is always profound. For more information, visit vday.org/organize.

Share Your Story. Ask for Help.

Violence against women is very much a silent epidemic in the United States, with sexual violence remaining one of the most underreported crimes. If you have been the victim of violence and/or abuse, reporting the crime and telling your story is a powerful tool in the fight to end violence against women and girls. Organizations exist that offer resources, support, facts, and counseling, so don't hesitate to reach out for help. In helping yourself heal, you can help bring the issue of violence to the forefront and let other women and girls know that they are not alone.

Volunteer

Donate time and/or resources to local organizations that address violence against women. You can volunteer at or donate to your local domestic violence shelter. Domestic violence shelters provide counseling and programs specifically designed to help victims of abuse move past their trauma and away from abusive relationships. Help ensure that these services are broadly accessible to underserved communities. Visit Feminist.com's Anti-Violence Resource Guide (www.feminist.com/antiviolence). This comprehensive guide features a wide range of listings, including emergency hotlines, national organizations against domestic violence, publications divided by topic, links to violence-against-women websites, and many other helpful resources.

Donate to V-Day

Join us; help V-Day enact its mission to raise awareness and funds to end violence against women and girls! Donate to V-Day at http://www.vday.org/donate.

Payments by check (make checks payable to V-Day) or credit card (with card number and expiration date) may also be sent to:

V-Day
303 Park Ave South
Suite 1184
New York, NY 10010-3657

Please include your name and address with all contributions. For additional information or to contribute by telephone, please call the V-Day administrative offices at 510-841-4025. (This number is for donations and administration only. For all other V-Day business, please call 212-645-8329.)

Sign Up for V-Mail

Get news of actions, opportunities, and performances, as well as the latest messages from Eve Ensler. Get involved, and stay involved: www.vday.org/vmail.

ACKNOWLEDGMENTS

We are deeply grateful and give thanks to the following people who helped us create this book:

ACLU Women's Rights Project
Altria Group
Avon
Lea Beresford
Diane Berry
Fran Berry
Carole Black
Kemery Bloom
The Bloomberg Foundation
Mama Cash
Deborah Colson
Katie Danzinger
Diana DeVegh
Abigail Disney
Cody Dobkins
Robert, Cynthia, and
    Erin Doyle
Laura Ensler
Jerri Lynn Fields
Eileen Fisher
The Ford Foundation
Robyn Goodman
Maris Goodstein
Judy and Walter Grossman
Patti Harris
Mellody Hobson
Cheryl and Ron Howard
I. Chera Sons Foundation
Julie Kavner
Lenora Lapidus

Deborah and John Larkin
Deborah Lee
Harriet N. Leve
Lisa Lopez
Elizabeth Maestre
Brian McClendon
Pat Mitchell
The New York Women's
    Foundation
Suze Orman
Purva Panday
Beth Pearson
Francie Pepper
Sarah Peter
Carol and Lisa Pittleman
Linda Pope
Abby Pogrebin
Emily Scott Pottruck
Allison Prouty
Marie Cecile Renauld
Anthony Romero
Nancy Rose
Jeffrey Seller
The Sister Fund
Howard and Sharon Socol
Starbucks
A'yen Tra
Urvashi Vaid
Verizon
Fran and Barry Weissler

And special thanks to:

The Rockefeller Foundation
Judith Rodin
Katherine McFate
Charlotte Sheedy
Nancy Miller

And to the V-Day Core: Susan Celia Swan, Cecile Lipworth, Kate Fisher, Tony Montenieri, Hibbaq Osman, Shael Norris, Hal Leventhal and Benita Kline, Selina Williams, Heather Moseley, and Amy Squires

ABOUT THE WRITERS

Writer-director ABIOLA ABRAMS uses movies and motivation to empower women under an initiative called the Goddess Factory. She is the host of BET's independent film series *The Best Shorts,* a short-film vehicle. Abrams's first novel, *Dare,* will be published by Simon & Schuster, and she is the creator of the Until the Violence Stops: NYC Women's Film Festival. She is a former producing host of HBO's politically incorrect interstitial *Chat Zone* and the syndicated NBC hip-hop news show *The Source.* Her award-winning artistic films investigate the themes of gender, race, and empowerment. Read more about her work at www.thegoddessfactory.com.

EDWARD ALBEE is the author of thirty plays, including *The Zoo Story; The Sandbox; The American Dream; Who's Afraid of Virginia Woolf?; A Delicate Balance; The Lady from Dubuque; Three Tall Women; The Play About the Baby; The Goat, or Who Is Sylvia?; Peter and Jerry;* and *Me, Myself and I.* He is a member of the Dramatists Guild Council and president of the Edward F. Albee Foundation. He has won three Pulitzer Prizes, four Tony Awards, the Kennedy Center Honors, and the National Medal of Arts. In 2005, he was awarded a Lifetime Achievement Tony Award.

TARIQ ALI is a novelist, historian, and playwright. He has written six novels and several plays (many in collaboration with Howard Brenton) as well as more than a dozen books on world history and politics. He is a long-standing editor of the *New Left Review* and lives in London.

MAYA ANGELOU is an American poet, memoirist, actress, and important figure in the American civil rights movement. Angelou is known for the autobiographical writings *I Know Why the Caged Bird Sings* (1969) and *All God's Children Need Traveling Shoes* (1986). Her volume of poetry *Just Give Me a Cool Drink of Water 'Fore I Die*

(1971) was nominated for the Pulitzer Prize, and in 1993 Angelou read her poem "On the Pulse of Morning" for Bill Clinton's presidential inauguration at his request.

PERIEL ASCHENBRAND is the author of the critically acclaimed book *The Only Bush I Trust Is My Own.* In 2003 she created and founded a T-shirt company called Body as Billboard (www.bodyas billboard.com). She has been the director of 401 Projects since April 2005.

PATRICIA BOSWORTH is an American journalist and biographer and a contributing editor for *Vanity Fair.* She is the author of the memoir *Anything Your Little Heart Desires: An American Family Story* and biographies of Montgomery Clift, Marlon Brando, and the photographer Diane Arbus. She is currently completing a biography of the actress and activist Jane Fonda.

NICOLE BURDETTE is an award-winning actress, playwright, and screenwriter. *Vogue* has called her "the Holly Golightly dramatist of New York City." As an actress, Burdette has appeared on stage and screen, most notably opposite Brad Pitt in Robert Redford's *A River Runs Through It* and most recently in a recurring role on *The Sopranos.* She wrote the screenplay adaptation of her play *Chelsea Walls,* and it premiered in 2002 at the Cannes Film Festival.

KATE CLINTON is a faith-based, tax-paying, American-loving political humorist and family entertainer. She has worked through economic booms and busts, Disneyfication and Wal-Martization, gay movements and gay markets, lesbian chic and queer eyes, and ten presidential inaugurals. She still believes that humor gets us through peacetime, wartime, and scoundrel time. In 2006 Clinton celebrates her twenty-fifth anniversary of performing with a fifty-city *It's Come to This!* tour across the United States and Canada. Her second book, *What the L?,* was nominated in the humor category for the prestigious 2005 Lambda Literary Award.

KIMBERLE CRENSHAW is a leading feminist theorist whose work is international in scope. A professor of law at UCLA and Columbia University, Crenshaw writes in the areas of civil rights, black feminist legal theory, and race. She coined the term "intersectionality" to examine converging oppression and the need to fight all "isms" simultaneously. As a media commentator on social justice issues such as violence against women and affirmative action, she has appeared on MSNBC and NPR's *Tavis Smiley Show*. She has also worked with the United Nations, the legal team representing Anita Hill, and the ACLU.

MICHAEL CUNNINGHAM's most recent novels are *The Hours* and *Specimen Days*.

EDWIDGE DANTICAT was born in Haiti and is the author of several books, including *Breath, Eyes, Memory; Krik? Krak!;* and *The Farming of Bones*. She is also the editor of *The Butterfly's Way: Voices from the Haitian Dyaspora in the United States* and *The Beacon Best of 2000: Great Writing by Men and Women of All Colors and Cultures* and has written two young adult novels, *Anacaona, Golden Flower* and *Behind the Mountains,* as well as a travel narrative, *After the Dance: A Walk Through Carnival in Jacmel*.

Chilean American ARIEL DORFMAN is a professor of literature at Duke University and has received numerous international awards, including the Sudamericana Award for Novel, the Olivier Award for Best Play (*Death and the Maiden,* which was made into a feature film by Roman Polanski), and two awards from the Kennedy Center. His books, written in both Spanish and English, have been translated into more than forty languages, and his plays have been staged in more than one hundred countries. Dorfman had three new plays produced in the 2005–6 season: *Purgatorio, The Other Side,* and *Picasso's Closet.* He also contributes regularly to the major newspapers of the world.

MOLLIE DOYLE works as a writer, editor, and producer. For the last ten years, she has had the privilege of working with Eve Ensler, first as the editor of *The Vagina Monologues*, and then as one of the dedicated people who support V-Day's mission to stop violence against women. Doyle has edited more than two hundred books and ghost-written several books; conceived, designed, and edited the magazine for the Harry Walker Agency, the world's largest speakers' bureau; and helped to produce major theatrical and television events around the world.

SLAVENKA DRAKULIĆ, born in Rijeka, Croatia (the former Yugoslavia) in 1949, is a writer and journalist whose work has been translated in many countries. She has published four novels: *Holograms of Fear, Marble Skin, The Taste of a Man,* and *S.: A Novel About the Balkans.* She has also published four nonfiction books: *How We Survived Communism and Even Laughed, The Balkan Express, Cafe Europa,* and *They Would Never Hurt a Fly: War Criminals on Trial in The Hague.* Her essays about the war in the Balkans have appeared in *The New Republic, The Nation, The New York Review of Books,* and other international newspapers and periodicals. She contributes to *Süddeutsche Zeitung* (Germany), *La Stampa* (Italy), *Dagens Nyheter* (Sweden), and *Politiken* (Denmark). She currently lives in Stockholm, Vienna, and Zagreb.

DR. MICHAEL ERIC DYSON was named by *Essence* magazine as one of the forty most inspiring African Americans and by *Ebony* magazine as one of the hundred most influential black Americans. In his thirteen books, Dyson has taken on some of the toughest and most controversial issues of our day. His latest book is *Debating Race.* His other books include *I May Not Get There with You, Holler If You Hear Me,* and *Come Hell or High Water.* Dyson has won the NAACP Image Award for *Why I Love Black Women* and *Is Bill Cosby Right? Or Has the Black Middle Class Lost Its Mind?* Dyson is the host of a syndicated radio show, *The Michael Eric Dyson Show.* He is the Avalon Foundation Professor in the Humanities and a professor of religious studies and Africana studies at the University of Pennsylvania.

DAVE EGGERS is the author of *A Heartbreaking Work of Staggering Genius, You Shall Know Our Velocity!, How We Are Hungry,* and *What Is the What.* In 1998 he founded McSweeney's, an independent publishing house, which now produces a quarterly literary journal, a monthly magazine, a daily humor website, and a DVD quarterly of short films. Eggers has also designed most of the books and periodicals published by McSweeney's. In 2002 he opened 826 Valencia, a writing lab for young people; there are now branches of 826 in San Francisco, New York, Los Angeles, Seattle, Chicago, and Michigan.

KATHY ENGEL is a poet, an essayist, an organizer, a producer, and a communications and creative consultant for social justice, peace, and human rights. She has co-founded numerous organizations, including MADRE, Riptide Communications, the Hayground School, KickAss-Artists, and East End Women in Black. She has co-produced and conceived of political cultural events and campaigns including Stand with Sisters for Economic Dignity; "Who's Gonna Be There?" a dramatic dialogue about mentors with Roy Scheider and Danny Glover; *Talking Nicaragua*; Moving Towards Home; "Who I Will Be"; and Imagining Peace. Her newest books are *Ruth's Skirts* (poems and prose) and *We Begin Here: Poems for Palestine and Lebanon* (co-edited by Kamal Boullata).

EVE ENSLER is a playwright, performer, and activist. Her award-winning play *The Vagina Monologues* has been translated into 45 languages and performed in more than 112 countries. Ensler's other plays include *Necessary Targets, Conviction, Lemonade, The Depot, Floating Rhoda and the Glue Man, Extraordinary Measures, The Good Body,* and *The Treatment.* Eve is also the author of *Insecure At Last: Losing It in a Security Obsessed World.* She is also the founder/artistic director of V-Day (www.vday.org), a global movement to end violence against women and girls, which has raised more than $40 million in nine years. She is the recipient of many honorary degrees and awards, including the Guggenheim Fellowship Award in Playwriting.

JANE FONDA's work on stage and screen has earned numerous nominations and awards, including Academy Awards for *Klute* and *Coming Home* and an Emmy for her performance in *The Dollmaker*. In addition to her acclaimed career as an actress, Fonda has also produced a number of her films, including *Coming Home, Nine to Five, The China Syndrome, On Golden Pond,* and *The Morning After*. Fonda revolutionized the fitness industry with her many workout books and videos. The original *Jane Fonda's Workout* video remains the top-grossing home video of all time. Long known for her activism and advocacy, Fonda now focuses much of her time on the organization she founded in 1995, the Georgia Campaign for Adolescent Pregnancy Prevention (G-CAPP), a statewide effort to eliminate teen pregnancy in Georgia. Fonda has also established the Jane Fonda Center for Adolescent Reproductive Health at the Emory University School of Medicine. The center engages in research, education, and training in adolescence and reproductive health. Fonda is a cofounder of the Women's Media Center and Greenstone Media.

CAROL GILLIGAN is the author of *In a Different Voice* and, most recently, *The Birth of Pleasure*. Her adaptation of *The Scarlet Letter* was presented in 2006 as part of the 2005 Women Center Stage festival and will be produced by the Culture Project next year. Her story "If I Forget Thee" was included in *110 Stories: New Yorkers Write After 9/11*. She initiated the Strengthening Healthy Resistance and Courage in Girls project and the Women Teaching Girls/Girls Teaching Women programs, was co–artistic director of the Company of Women, an all-woman theater troupe, and is currently a professor at New York University. She dedicates her monologue "My House Is Wallpapered with Lies" to the eleven-year-old girls whose voices inspired it.

JYLLIAN GUNTHER is an Emmy Award–winning writer and director. Her critically acclaimed documentary *Pullout* was an official selection at film festivals, including Hamptons, Raindance UK, Newport, and Mill Valley. She also developed a series based on *Pullout* for New York Times Television/TLC. Most recently, she directed multiple episodes of the Emmy-nominated PBS series *Postcards from Buster*; a

PSA series for PBS (writer/director Emmy, 2002); MTV's *Made*; Noggin's *Love High* (an original pilot); and the CBS/Nickelodeon/Bill Cosby series *Little Bill*. She was a staff writer at Nickelodeon and freelances for IFC, AMC, WE, Oxygen, and others. Her plays have been produced in New York, Los Angeles, and San Francisco. She's currently directing a documentary about the inaugural four years of a small public high school in Bed-Stuy, Brooklyn. You can visit her website at www.wonderful6inc.com.

SUHEIR HAMMAD is the author of *Born Palestinian, Born Black, Drops of This Story,* and *Zaatar Diva*. She is an original writer and performer in the Tony Award–winning *Russell Simmons Presents Def Poetry Jam* on Broadway, and has appeared on every season of HBO's *Def Poetry Jam*. She was awarded the Women of Color Resource Center's Sister of Fire Award in 2005.

CHRISTINE HOUSE got involved with V-Day through her performance in *The Vagina Monologues* in Littleton, Massachusetts, but was drafted into the fight to end violence against women long before the movement had a name. Thank you to Eve Ensler for giving it one! She is honored to be part of this festival.

MARIE HOWE: B.S., University of Windsor. M.F.A., Columbia University. Poet; author of *The Good Thief,* selected by Margaret Atwood for the National Poetry Series; editor, with Michael Klein, of *In the Company of My Solitude: American Writing from the AIDS Pandemic;* author of *What the Living Do;* recipient of the Peter I. B. Lavan Younger Poet Award from the Academy of American Poets, the Mary Ingram Bunting Fellowship from Radcliffe College, and grants from the National Endowment for the Arts, the Massachusetts Artist Foundation, and the Guggenheim. Faculty member at Sarah Lawrence since 1993.

CAROL MICHÈLE KAPLAN's plays have been produced in the United States and South Africa and have garnered numerous awards, as has her film and television writing. She has an M.F.A. from the Yale School of Drama, a J.D. from New York University School of Law, and is a member of the Writers Guild of America. Her most recent play, *Bot,* was awarded an Alfred P. Sloane Foundation grant and will be produced by the Magic Theatre in San Francisco.

MOISÉS KAUFMAN is an award-winning writer and director. His plays *Gross Indecency: The Three Trials of Oscar Wilde* and *The Laramie Project* have been among the most honored and most widely performed plays in America over the last decade. Selected directing credits include the Pulitzer- and Tony Award–winning play *I Am My Own Wife, Macbeth* (Shakespeare in the Park), *This Is How It Goes* (Donmar Warehouse), and the HBO film version of *The Laramie Project,* which opened the 2002 Sundance Film Festival. Kaufman is the founder and artistic director of Tectonic Theater Project, a laboratory for new works in theater and film. He is the recipient of the Joe A. Callaway Award for directing and a Guggenheim Fellowship in playwriting.

MICHAEL KLEIN has written *Track Conditions,* a memoir; *The End of Being Known,* a book of essays; and *1990,* a book of poems. He is currently writing a book of essays called *When I Was a Twin,* and recent work is forthcoming in the journal *Bloom.* He lives in New York and teaches every summer at the Fine Arts Work Center in Provincetown, Massachusetts.

NICHOLAS D. KRISTOF is a columnist for *The New York Times.* In 1990 Kristof and his wife, Sheryl WuDunn, also a *Times* journalist, won a Pulitzer Prize for their coverage of China's Tiananmen Square democracy movement. They were the first married couple to win a Pulitzer for journalism. Kristof has also won the George Polk Award, the Overseas Press Club award, the Michael Kelly award, the Online News Association award, and the American Society of Newspaper Editors award. In 2006 he won a second Pulitzer, for commentary. Kristof and WuDunn are the authors of *China Wakes* and *Thunder from the East.*

JAMES LECESNE created the critically acclaimed *Word of Mouth,* directed by Eve Ensler and produced by Mike Nichols. His film

Trevor won an Academy Award and inspired the Trevor Project, a nonprofit organization that operates the only twenty-four-hour suicide prevention helpline for GLBT and Questioning teens. Working with young people in Cambodia, Tibet, and Bosnia, Lecesne created *The Road Home: Stories of Children of War,* which was presented at the International Peace Initiative at The Hague. He also adapted Armistead Maupin's *Further Tales of the City* for Showtime and wrote one of the final episodes of the TV series *Will & Grace.* His novel, *Absolute Brightness,* will be published in the fall of 2007.

ELIZABETH LESSER is the co-founder of Omega Institute (www. eomega.org), America's largest adult education center focusing on health, spirituality, and creativity. She is the author of *The Seeker's Guide* and *Broken Open: How Difficult Times Can Help Us Grow.* For the past four years, she and Eve Ensler have spearheaded the Women and Power conferences—electrifying dialogues among women activists, artists, and leaders from around the world. Formerly a midwife and birth educator, she teaches workshops on emotional intelligence, grief and loss, and meditation, and she lectures at colleges, retreat centers, and conferences nationwide.

MARK MATOUSEK is the author of two acclaimed memoirs: *Sex Death Enlightenment: A True Story,* an international bestseller published in ten countries, and *The Boy He Left Behind: A Man's Search for His Lost Father.* A contributing editor to *O: The Oprah Magazine, Tricycle,* and *Out,* and a former editor at *Interview* magazine, Matousek is the co-author (with Andrew Harvey) of *Dialogues with a Modern Mystic;* editor of *Still Here* by Ram Dass, a National Magazine Award nominee; and winner of a 2001 Triangle award for nonfiction. His new book, *The Roar of Freedom,* will be published in 2008.

DEENA METZGER is a novelist, poet, essayist, storyteller, and healer. Her books include *From Grief into Vision: A Council, Entering the Ghost River: Meditations on the Theory and Practice of Healing, Tree: Essays & Pieces,* and *Writing for Your Life: A Guide and Companion to the Inner Worlds.* She co-edited *Intimate Nature: The*

Bond Between Women and Animals. Her novels include *The Other Hand, What Dinah Thought,* and *Doors: A Fiction for Jazz Horn.* Her most recent books of poetry are *Looking for the Faces of God* and *A Sabbath Among the Ruins. New and Selected Poems* will be published in 2008.

SUSAN MILLER is an award-winning playwright and Guggenheim Fellow whose works include the critically acclaimed one-woman play *My Left Breast,* for which she won an Obie; *A Map of Doubt and Rescue,* which earned her the Susan Smith Blackburn Prize and the Pinter Prize for Drama; and *Nasty Rumors and Final Remarks,* also an Obie winner. Other plays: *For Dear Life; Flux; Confessions of a Female Disorder; It's Our Town, Too;* and *The Grand Design.* She has been produced at the Public Theater, Second Stage, Actors Theatre of Louisville, Naked Angels, and the Mark Taper Forum, among others. Miller has also written for *O: The Oprah Magazine* and was a consulting producer on Showtime's hit series *The L Word.*

WINTER MILLER is a playwright. Her play *In Darfur* has been developed by the Guthrie Theater, the Public Theater, the Geva Theater, and the Playwrights Center. Miller has traveled with Nicholas D. Kristof to the Sudan border to interview genocide survivors. Her plays include *The Penetration Play,* which was published by Playscripts, Inc., and excerpted in Smith & Kraus's *Best Stage Scenes 2005* and *Best Monologues 2005; Conspicuous; Something's Wrong with Amandine;* and *Cake and Ice Cream.* Miller has also written for *The New York Times.* A graduate of Smith College, she holds an M.F.A. from Columbia University and is a member of the Obie-winning 13Playwrights.

SUSAN MINOT is the author of *Monkeys, Lust & Other Stories, Folly, Evening, Rapture,* and a poetry collection, *Poems 4 A.M.* She wrote the screenplay for Bernardo Bertolucci's *Stealing Beauty.* Minot lives with her husband and daughter on North Haven, an island in Maine, and occasionally in New York City. "They Took All of Us" was created from an interview with Sister Rachele in Uganda conducted in 1998. All the words are hers.

An award-winning writer, feminist leader, political theorist, journalist, and editor, ROBIN MORGAN has published more than twenty books, including six of poetry, four of fiction, and the now-classic anthologies *Sisterhood Is Powerful, Sisterhood Is Global,* and *Sisterhood Is Forever.* A founder of contemporary U.S. feminism, she has also been a leader in the international women's movement for twenty-five years. Recent books include *Saturday's Child: A Memoir;* her bestselling *The Demon Lover: The Roots of Terrorism;* her new novel, *The Burning Time;* and her nonfiction *Fighting Words: A Toolkit for Combating the Religious Right* (www.robinmorgan.us).

KATHY NAJIMY was voted *Ms.* magazine's 2005 Woman of the Year. She starred as Mae West in *Dirty Blonde* on Broadway and wrote and starred off-Broadway in *The Kathy and Mo Show,* which won an Obie Award and was filmed for two HBO specials, which won Ace Awards. Najimy provides the voice of Peggy Hill on *King of the Hill,* starred on NBC's *Veronica's Closet,* and was thrilled to play Sharon Stone's gynecologist in *If These Walls Could Talk 2.* Najimy has appeared in more than twenty films, including *Hocus Pocus, Rat Race,* and *Say Uncle,* and is internationally known as Sister Mary Patrick in the hit films *Sister Act* and *Sister Act 2: Back in the Habit.* She has been published in *The New York Times* and in the books *Choices We Made, If You Had Five Minutes with the President,* and *Starpower.* She has been honored for her activism with AIDS, choice, gay rights, Arabic pride, and women's rights. She is proud to be one of the founding members of V-Day. Najimy lives in Los Angeles with her husband, Dan Finnerty (of the Dan Band), and their glorious daughter, Samia.

LYNN NOTTAGE's plays include *A Stone's Throw/The Antigone Project* (The Women's Project), *Fabulation or, the Re-Education* (Playwrights Horizons, Tricycle Theatre), and *Intimate Apparel* (Roundabout Theatre Company, Mark Taper Forum, South Coast Rep, Center Stage, among others). Her awards include: Lucille Lortel Playwriting Award, Obie Award, New York Drama Critics Circle, Outer Critics Circle Awards, American Theatre Critics/Steinberg, Francesca Primus, AUDELCO, National Black Theatre Festival's August

Wilson Playwriting Award, 2004 PEN/Laura Pels Award, and a Guggenheim Fellowship. She is a resident member of New Dramatists and a visiting lecturer at the Yale School of Drama and Princeton University.

SHARMEEN OBAID-CHINOY is a multiple award-winning documentary filmmaker. Obaid-Chinoy was raised in Karachi, Pakistan, and educated at Smith College and Stanford University. She began her career in 2002 with New York Times Television; since then she has produced and reported on more than nine documentary films.

SHARON OLDS is a professor of English at New York University. She is one of the country's most lauded poets and the author of *Blood, Tin, Straw; The Wellspring; The Father; The Gold Cell; The Dead and the Living;* and *Satan Says.* Her fellowship honors include the T. S. Eliot Prize shortlist for *The Father,* 1994; Lila Wallace–Reader's Digest Writer's Award, 1993–96; and the National Book Critics Circle Award for *The Dead and The Living,* 1984. Chancellor, the Academy of American Poets, fellow of the American Academy of Arts and Science.

HANAN AL-SHAYKH was born in Lebanon and grew up in Beirut. Her most recent novel, *Only in London,* was shortlisted for the Independent Foreign Fiction Prize. She was educated in Cairo and wrote her first novel there when she was nineteen, before returning to Beirut to work as a journalist for *Annahar* newspaper and *Al-Hasnaa* magazine. Al-Shaykh writes in Arabic, and although her novels were initially banned in many Arab countries for their sexual explicitness, her work has been translated into twenty-one languages and is now published around the world. Al-Shaykh is widely regarded as one of the foremost experts on Arab womanhood. Her latest work is a story about the life of her mother, *Hikayati Sharhun Yatool.*

ANNA DEAVERE SMITH is an actress and a writer. She is said to have developed a new form of theater. She interviews people and performs them in one-person shows, looking at societal and human issues from multiple points of view. She has performed up to forty-six characters in the same show. Awards include two Obies, two Tony nominations and the MacArthur Award. She played national security adviser Nancy McNally on *The West Wing* and acts in films. She is the founding director of the Institute on the Arts and Civic Dialogue and teaches at New York University.

MONICA SZLEKOVICS (Inmate97G1571). I am a woman who is both victim and offender. I am a woman to whom very few accolades are given. I am a woman who was essentially groomed to become a heroin addict at sixteen who eventually met and became involved with a violent man. I am a woman who is seeking out her own truths. I am a woman who is exploring, accepting, and reconciling with her past. I am a woman who is actively trying to stop perpetuating the cycle of violence in her life. I am more than just a number, the consequences of my disempowerment. I have a history. I have a voice, and I am not unlike you. I am Monica Szlekovics, a thirty-year-old woman who now refuses to be demeaned, exploited, and mistreated.

ROBERT THURMAN is the Jey Tsong Khapa Professor of Indo-Tibetan Buddhist Studies in the Department of Religion at Columbia University; president of the Tibet House U.S., a nonprofit dedicated to the preservation and promotion of Tibetan civilization; and president of the American Institute of Buddhist Studies, a nonprofit dedicated to the publication of translations of important texts from the Tibetan Tanjur. *Time* magazine chose Thurman as one of its twenty-five most influential Americans in 1997. He is the author of many books, including *Inner Revolution, Worlds of Transformation,* and *Infinite Life,* and translator of the Tibetan Book of the Dead.

BETTY GALE TYSON was incarcerated for twenty-five years (to the day) for a crime she didn't commit. She credits her sanity and survival to the Bible and her mother. In 1998 she was exonerated and released from Bedford Hills Correctional Facility for Women. The state of New York has yet to apologize for taking away twenty-five years of her life. Tyson's mother died six months after she got out. She lives to honor her mother's spirit, so she spends much of her time speaking about this experience.

ALICE WALKER is one of the most prolific and important writers of our time, known for her literary fiction, including the Pulitzer Prize–winning *The Color Purple* (now a major Broadway play), her many volumes of poetry, and her powerful nonfiction collections. Walker has also published several children's books. *There Is a Flower at the Tip of My Nose Smelling Me* is her most recent work for children and adults. In the fall of 2006 she published a book of spiritual ruminations with a progressive political edge: *We Are the Ones We Have Been Waiting For: Inner Light in a Time of Darkness.*

In 1997, JODY WILLIAMS became the tenth woman in the Nobel Peace Prize's nearly hundred-year history to be awarded the prize for her work with the International Campaign to Ban Landmines. She continues to serve as campaign ambassador. In 2006, she took the lead in co-founding the Nobel Women's Initiative with five other women Peace Laureates to defend the rights of women around the world. Williams is also a Distinguished Visiting Professor at the University of Houston's Graduate College of Social Work. A writer, speaker, and activist, Jody Williams is an outspoken advocate for human rights and human security as the basis for international peace and security.

ERIN CRESSIDA WILSON is a writer and professor in the Literary Arts Program at Brown University. She won the 2003 Independent Spirit Award for her screenplay *Secretary,* starring James Spader and Maggie Gyllenhaal. She also wrote the film *Fur,* starring Nicole Kidman and Robert Downey, Jr., directed by Steven Shainberg. Her twenty plays have been produced regionally, off-Broadway and abroad. With Lillian Ann Slugocki, she co-authored *The Erotica Project,* produced at Joe's Pub and published by Cleis Press. She is a graduate of Smith College.

HOWARD ZINN was a shipyard worker, then an air force bombardier. He received his Ph.D. in history at Columbia University, and taught for seven years at Spelman College in Atlanta, where he became involved in the civil rights movement. He later taught at Boston

University, and has been a visiting professor in Paris and Bologna. He was active in the movement against the Vietnam War. Among his many books is the bestselling *A People's History of the United States.* His plays *Emma* (about Emma Goldman) and *Marx in Soho* have been produced in the U.S. and abroad.